YOU CAN WIN OVER WEARINESS

W. Ross Foley

A Division of G/L Publications
Glendale, California, U.S.A.

Dedicated affectionately
to the congregation of
Faith Convenant Church
Burnsville, Minnesota,
who bless me constantly
with affirmation and love.

Other good Regal reading:
   Your Churning Place by Robert Wise
   Joy All the Way by Stanley Collins
   Always a Winner by Cyril J. Barber
      and John D. Carter
   Who Are the Happy? by E.M. Blaiklock
   Love Unlimited by Festo Kivengere

Published by Regal Books Division, G/L Publications
Glendale, California 91209
Printed in U.S.A.
Library of Congress Catalog Card No. 77-90585
ISBN 0-8307-0586-4

══CONTENTS══

≡ACKNOWLEDGMENTS≡

Apart from Jesus, Himself, the person in the New Testament whom I admire most is Joseph, whose friends nicknamed him *Barnabas*, meaning "son of encouragement" (Acts 4:36). No one was ever more suitably named. For, wherever we meet him in the Acts of the Apostles, Barnabas is always "coming along side" others to help, enable, encourage, exhort and empower them in some vital way.

My admiration for Barnabas stems from my relationship with people who have been a Barnabas to me. Indeed, the very existence of this book is a case in point. Originally, the following chapters were messages delivered to the congregation of Faith Covenant Church in Burnsville, Minnesota. While many people responded exuberantly to those messages, one man in particular took the initiative to get them published. For several years, Ted Larson has urged me to seek wider circulation for some of my material. When I failed to pursue his suggestion, he took matters into his own hands. Eventually he caught the attention of Lloyd Ahlem, who recommended the material to Fritz Ridenour at Regal Books, who was gracious enough to publish it.

Other "Barnabases" who have played a key role in this project are my secretary, Grace Feuk, who typed the original manuscript from my illegible handwriting, and Marge Carlson, a friend who retyped the material for publication. I am happy to add that my wife, Rae Ann, is the number one Barnabas in my life. The Lord uses her daily ministry of encouragement and affirmation to lift my spirit and to replenish my staying power.

As you read this book, I pray that the Holy Spirit will "come along side" you, helping, enabling, encouraging, exhorting and empowering you to hang in there. May He send into your life many Barnabases who believe in you and who communicate that trust in ways that affirm and enable you.

≡INTRODUCTION≡

Our congregation had just completed its steward-
ship thrust for another year. I had poured every
ounce of energy into that campaign. Our church was
on the verge of a great new surge. My expectations
were sky-high. So, in my naive idealism, I waited
eagerly for our people to respond to the word God
had spoken to them and to the dreams we had shared
with them.

But as I watched their faith-promises dribble in, I
saw our dream dying. And as our dream died, I died
with it—a slow, painful death of depression and
disappointment. My depression became so intense I
could neither work nor think. I wrote no new messages during those weeks, for I had nothing to say
that they would want to hear. So I resorted to "old
stuff" from the past. I was whipped, totally defeated.

Finally, on the brink of despair, I spent the better
part of an afternoon in prayer, pouring my heart out
to God, then to my wife. And out of that experience
came some insights from God and from her that I
want to share with you in this book. Oh, the problem
didn't disappear. Far from it. But out of the ashes of
those dark days came the strength to hang in there.

1
YOU GOTTA HAVE HEART

And let us not grow weary in well-doing, for in due season we shall reap, if we do not lose heart (Gal. 6:9).

Weariness, fatigue and the temptation to quit are no strangers to any of us. Some of us are troubled by the suspicion that our spiritual go has got up and went. Some time ago, I delivered a message on the elder brother of the prodigal son, a message in which I invited our parishioners to "'Come to the Party"[1] at the Father's house and enjoy the feast and festivities of His grace. At the conclusion of that celebration, one of our key leaders said to me: "What about those of us who are always working at the party? How can we enjoy the feast when we are so busy serving the guests?"

Now there is the voice of weariness, the echo of exasperation, the witness of someone who is working more now and enjoying it less. She was tired of the ongoing battle of discipleship. Her spiritual go had got up and went. In other words, she was dangerously close to growing weary in well-doing.

Hazardous to Your Health

Burnout is the heavy hazard that dogs the steps of people-helpers. Weariness is the price the sower often pays, especially when the harvest is delayed far beyond the expected date. It is great to be a front-runner in the cause of Christ. But front-runners pay the price of fatigue. They are tempted to grow weary in well-doing. They grow tired of the trivia and trials that plague leadership; trivia and trials their followers know little about. This may be where you find yourself. God has saved you by His grace, has given you certain gifts, has opened the door to a particular ministry where your gifts can be expressed, and has commissioned you to get involved. You have obeyed Him and are now giving yourself to the task at hand.

Yours may be a ministry of teaching a class, counseling a youth group, administrating a board, serving on a committee, using your musical talents, leading a group, conducting a Bible study, caring for people who cannot care for themselves, evangelizing unbelievers, taking leadership in civic and political affairs, living for Christ in a pagan world. Or, your main ministry at present may be in your home nurturing and training your children and loving your husband.

Whatever your ministry may be, your faithful pursuit of it will expose you to grave danger—the danger of growing weary in well-doing. Front-runners are susceptible to high risk—the risk of fatigue. People who plant God's good seed of love in the lives of others expend enormous amounts of energy doing so.

Even a ministry so "routine" as being a good wife, mother and homemaker is proving to be an extremely high-risk vocation today.

The crisis facing the American family in the 1960s and early '70s was the flight of teenagers. By the hundreds of thousands teenagers were running away from home each year. Now those doing the running are wives and mothers, especially young mothers. Young mothers who spend every waking hour planting and sowing good seed in the lives of their children, and who are so many years removed from the harvest, are despairing of their roles and running away. This is a growing, scary phenomenon haunting America in the '70s.

Because of my recent experience of this temptation to run, and because I sense that some of you may have tired blood, sagging spirits and weary souls, I want to devote these pages to what the Bible has to say about weariness, its causes and cures. The Scriptures show us how we can win over weariness. That good word comes through loud and clear, without pious platitudes or success slogans. Just powerful principles that really work in daily living if we are willing to work them.

The *New Yorker* magazine carried a cartoon depicting a group of convicts huddled in a circle on the floor of their cell block. Spread out before them was a map of the prison grounds, and on the map a detailed route for their planned escape. One of the prisoners turned to the leader of the group and said, "I wish you wouldn't keep saying, 'This is where we are now.' "[2]

We share that prisoner's frustration. We have a

9

pretty good idea where we are now. So let's get on with it. Let's stop reminding ourselves where we are and concentrate on where we want to be. We want to break out of our prison of fatigue and beat back the dangers of weariness. So away we go!

Any consideration of the Bible's antidote for weariness must start with the classic text on the subject, Galatians 6:9, "And let us not grow weary in well-doing, for in due season we shall reap, if we do not lose heart."

Paul issues this exhortation in the first person plural, "let us," thereby including himself. By so doing he confesses that he, too, is exposed to the grave danger of growing weary in well-doing. No one is exempt from this risk. To help you understand what Paul means by this statement, let me begin by showing you what he doesn't mean.

Depression Can Be Friendly

There is a difference between depression and despair. A good bit of our weariness is misunderstood and exaggerated because we mistake depression for despair, but they are very different dimensions of life. It is imperative that you view depression as your friend. Depression can be a healthy friend in three vital ways.

First, the experience of depression is friendly when it is the only healthy response to one of life's crises. Allen Stark was 40 when his father died suddenly of a heart attack. As the shock waned, he found himself wanting to be alone, waking in the night, remembering and crying. His wife, who had always considered Allen the epitome of stability was frightened by the

10

expression of his feelings. As weeks passed she became increasingly critical of him. "Haven't you cried enough?" she insisted. To which Allen replied, "How much is enough?" It took Allen nearly six months to recover fully from the impact of his father's death. Yet afterwards he described himself as "better put-together than before."[3]

Few people are as open about their feelings of depression as Allen Stark. Being depressed is still considered a weakness and a source of embarrassment to most people. Most of us prefer to ignore signs of depression. But the truth of the matter is: the only healthy response to many situations in life, such as loss or grief, is depression. Not to be depressed after a serious loss is to be sick. The key to whether our depression is healthy or sick is whether its intensity and duration correspond to the severity of the crisis we are experiencing. Failing a vital examination or losing a crucial game should induce depression of short duration. But going through the life-wrenching stress of a divorce may induce a period of depression lasting many months. Both short and lengthy experiences of depression can be your friend when they are the only healthy response to the crisis you are facing.

Second, the experience of depression is friendly when it balances the experience of euphoria in our lives. All of us have a median line of normalcy in our personality. Above and below that line our moods swing to heights of elation and depths of gloom. Some of us have relatively little swing in our moods. We never get very "high" and never very "low." That kind of level pattern makes us rather dull, flat personalities. But others swing to the mountaintops of euphoria and then plummet to the valleys of depression.

The point is that our highs will always be matched by our lows. We will never swing further above the plane of normalcy in our personality than we swing below it. When we are riding high on the wings of elation and euphoria, we are burning high-octane energy and are taxing all of our emotional faculties to the limit. Therefore, we cannot handle an endless succession of highs. For that reason our personality seeks balance by swinging to an equal distance below the plane of normalcy. Consequently a high experience of euphoria is followed by a low experience of depression. And that low experience of acute, painful, intense, short-lived depression can be very healthy as our body, mind and spirit take time-out to recover the energy expended on the mountaintop of elation.

Third, the experience of depression is friendly when it sounds a warning in our lives that something is wrong. Depression is not a disease. It is a symptom like a fever or a sensation of pain. An experience of depression—especially prolonged, abnormal depression—may be a symptom that something is wrong with us physically, psychologically and/or spiritually. Thus as a symptom, depression sounds the alarm that all is not well with us. In a different context, C.S. Lewis put it like this:

> God whispers to us in our pleasures, speaks
> in our conscience, but shouts in our pain; it
> is His megaphone to rouse a deaf world.[4]

In that sense, our experiences of depression can be very friendly. When they become God's attention-getters, forcing us to seek His face and respond to His will, to thrust ourselves on His mercy and to make ourselves attentive to Him, they are indeed most friendly.

That is exactly what my recent experience of darkness forced me to do. It was God's gracious way of getting my attention. I had been trusting in my ability to motivate people. My failure refocused my sights on the one whom I should have been trusting. For that reason, my depression was a true and dear friend.

Now it is important to note that the experience of healthy depression is not the issue at stake in Galatians 6:9. Paul is not addressing himself to the normal cycle of life's ups and downs with their elation and depression, euphoria and disappointment. He is talking to human beings. Therefore, he cannot commission us never to become depressed or disappointed with life and its stress. On the contrary, he is speaking of something far more serious than our friendly bouts with depression. The deadly enemy to which he is referring is *despair*.

Despair Is Deadly

Everything we have just said about depression is designed to stand in bold contrast to what we are going to say about despair. Whereas depression is friendly, despair is deadly. Despair results from depression that is handled in an unhealthy manner—depression that has gone to seed.

When we dip down into the occasional ditch of depression, we must make sure that we drain the swamps of self-pity, grumbling, anger and bitterness. For if we do not drain those disease-inducing swamps, if we nurse self-pity, anger and bitterness, we allow our depression to transform itself into despair. The results are that we move from the friendly to the deadly. For, to despair is to give up hope, to throw in the towel, to quit. That is the danger about which the apostle Paul is so exercised in Galatians 6:9.

Paul uses two very strong words to communicate the urgency of his exhortation. The word *weary* literally means "to despair, to give in to difficulty, to throw in the towel and quit." And the phrase *lose heart* means to "abandon the effort, to loosen one's belt and retire from action."

The imagery in Paul's mind was that of a first-century farmer out planting the seed in his fields. Since men of ancient times wore long, flowing robes it became necessary to gather those robes tightly around their waists and tie them there whenever they engaged in strenuous physical activity. Hence, the New Testament talk about "girding up your loins" meant to batten down every possible encumbrance and free yourself from every distraction.

However, to "lose heart" is to do just the opposite. To "lose heart" means to loosen your belt and walk off the job, abandon the effort, give in to difficulty, yield to despair. That is the second strong temptation Satan presses upon the people of God. Paul alludes to the primary temptation in Galatians 6:7,8. Satan tempts us first to "sow to our flesh," to live our lives selfishly, indulgently, willfully, pursuing the desires of the flesh and the works of our own selfish designs. But we can allow God to offset that temptation by His power in our lives. We can choose to "sow to the

Spirit," to yield ourselves totally to Jesus and to make ourselves available to His beck and call, receiving His love, running His errands, doing His will, sharing His love and power with people around us, becoming involved in their hurts and cares.

But even if we choose to "sow to the Spirit" rather than "to the flesh," the battle is not over. It has merely begun. For then the enemy focuses his attack on our endurance. He prompts us to despair, to give in to difficulty, to throw in the towel, to loosen our belts and walk off the job, abandoning the effort, giving up hope. The temptation to despair is Satan's second great temptation for a Christian. And if he succeeds in getting us to walk off the job, he wins a momentous triumph and thrusts a terrible tragedy upon us—we lose our share in the harvest.

The Harvest Is Coming

Our good works done in the name and by the power of Jesus are going to reap a tremendous harvest someday. People are being helped and healed and changed and encouraged and blessed beyond our fondest dreams by our "well-doing." Great praise and glory are ascending to God the Father and the Son as a result of every effort we are making and every ministry we are performing by the enabling power of the Holy Spirit. The harvest is coming! There will be a jubilant day of reaping someday.

But only those who endure to the end will share in the harvest. Paul makes it very clear that we will reap only "if we do not lose heart." Endurance is the condition for reaping. Those who grow weary in well-doing and lose heart, lose their share in the harvest.

Therefore, God's Word to us is: "You gotta have heart." You've got to receive His enabling love so you can hang in there.

Servants with Staying Power

When we study the lives of God's people, great or small, we find one predominant characteristic marking all of them. They all have staying power. They all have found the strength to hang tough against the most impossible odds.

Adoniram Judson, Christendom's pioneer missionary to Burma, had staying power. Judson went buzzing off to Burma, the first to take the good news of Christ to that Moslem country. But when he stepped on their shores and started his mission of mercy, they threw him in jail. And he became depressed, woefully depressed. He lay there thinking of how useless he was, and how useful he could have been had he heeded the counsel of his friends and stayed in the West where many congregations clamored for his ministry.

But though he became depressed and discouraged, Judson did not let his depression degenerate into despair. He drained the swamps of self-pity and bitterness and let God use those "useless" months to teach him lessons he could learn in no other way. Finally the day came when those prison doors were opened. And Adoniram Judson walked out into the countryside of Burma, a man armed with the staying power of Jesus Christ. History tells of the thousands upon thousands of pagan peoples of Burma whose lives were transformed by the power of Christ coming through a servant who wouldn't give up.[5]

Rowland Bingham had the same kind of staying

16

power. He heard God's call to the interior of Africa at a time when no other white man dared set foot on that soil. He responded to that call and prepared to go. No missionary board would accept him. But that did not stop him. No church would support him. But that did not stop him. He hopped a freighter with two friends and worked his way to Egypt. Then they purchased supplies and struck off into the interior of Africa. He contracted malaria. But that did not stop him. His two companions gave up and abandoned the effort. But that did not stop him.

Bingham went on alone. For the first 14 years of his missionary ministry (seven years getting to the field and seven years on the field), there was not one conversion to Jesus Christ. People back home who received word of his fruitless efforts told him he was crazy to stay. But that did not stop him. He stayed, though he too became discouraged and wondered what God was doing with him in such a desolate place. But Rowland Bingham had staying power. He refused to despair. He did not lose heart. As a result, he lived to share in the harvest of many thousands whose lives were changed by the power of Christ.

Today, the Sudan Interior Mission, one of Christianity's most successful missionary agencies in Africa, stands as the shadow of one man's staying power—Rowland Bingham—the man who would not give up on the God who had called him.[6]

That is the kind of commitment to which Paul is calling us today. "Let us not grow weary [despair, throw in the towel] in well-doing, for in due season we shall reap, if we do not lose heart [loosen our belts, walk off the job and abandon the effort]." Experiences of depression and discouragement will come. That is normal. Our experiences of depression and discouragement can be very friendly. But they can become deadly if we let them turn into despair.

When you are down in the valley of depression, thrust yourself upon the Lord. Drain the swamps of self-pity, bitterness, anger and resentment. Don't despair! Don't grow weary in well-doing. Don't lose heart. For if you do, you will lose your share in the harvest. The harvest is coming! So whatever you do, don't lose your share of the harvest. Get with God. Go with Him. Stay with Him in faithful planting. And you will enjoy His harvest.

Notes

1. The title was taken from Karl Olsson's *Come to the Party*, (Waco: Word Books, 1972).
2. Warren Hamby, *Winds of Change*. Quoted in *My Third Reader's Notebook*, compiled by Gerald Kennedy (Nashville: Abingdon Press, 1974), p. 83.
3. Frederic Flach, "The Secret Strength of Depression." *Family Circle*, May 1975, p. 20.
4. C.S. Lewis, *The Problem of Pain* (New York: Macmillan Publishing Company, Inc., 1962), p. 93.
5. John Pollock, *Victims of the Long March* (Waco: Word Books, 1970), pp. 21–29.
6. Pollock, *Victims*, pp. 81–88.

2
REST FOR THE RESTLESS

> Come to me, all who labor and are heavy laden, and I will give you rest (Matt. 11:28).

These words of Jesus from Matthew 11 find their closest parallel in the poem of Emma Lazarus inscribed on the Statue of Liberty:

> Give me your tired, your poor,
> Your huddled masses yearning to breathe
>   free,
> The wretched refuse of your teeming shore.
> Send these, the homeless, tempest
>   tossed to me,
> I lift my lamp beside the golden door![1]

Indeed, Jesus was addressing His invitation to the tired, poor, huddled masses yearning to breathe free. He was speaking to the common people of the land in which He lived, people who were trying desperately to be good enough to please God, but who were finding that goal impossible to achieve. Their religious leaders had laid upon their shoulders the heavy

19

burden of legalism. They had been taught that the way to impress God was to live a good moral life, to keep an endless assortment of rules and regulations.

So the average citizen of the land was conscientiously trying to make his way through a maze of "Thou shalt nots." He was stumbling and fumbling through a forest of rules. Yet try as he did, he could not measure up to the mark his religion set before him. Consequently, life for the man in the street had become tedious and oppressive, filled with an immobilizing sense of guilt and frustration. He had been driven to weariness and despair by the sheer impossibility of living up to the demands of his religion.

So it was to the conscientious common people of the land, to people of good intentions and lofty motives, to people who were trying to live good, moral lives, to people who were frustrated by the futility of their efforts and the reality of their failures that Jesus said, "Come to me, all who labor and are heavy laden, and I will give you rest."

Do-It-Yourself Religion

Labor literally means "weariness, exhaustion." *Heavy laden* means "overwhelmed with an impossible burden." Therefore, Jesus is inviting all who are weary, exhausted and overwhelmed by the burden of a do-it-yourself religion. And He promises that all who come to Him will receive rest for their weary souls and relief from their troubled consciences.

The Bible makes it abundantly clear that there is no weariness in all the world like the fatigue experienced by well-intentioned, zealous, conscientious people of good works who attempt to attract God's attention, gain His approval, win His favor and balance their ledger by the rules they keep, the rituals they observe and the good moral lives they lead. According to the Scriptures, people who are trapped on the treadmill of do-it-yourself religion are of all people the most exhausted, most weary, most miserable.

If John Wesley were alive today, he would testify that "trying to be good" overwhelms the do-it-your-selfer with oppression and wearies him with disillusionment.

At the age of 22, Wesley's conscience began to awaken to the stirrings of religious zeal. So he set himself to a rigorous pursuit of Bible reading, prayer and severe discipline so that he might be saved on the basis of "not being as bad as others."

Wesley enrolled at Oxford University, cut himself off from all questionable companions and joined "the Holy Club," a group of highly dedicated, extremely disciplined, devout young men whose consuming passion was to measure up to God's standards and win His favor.

In October, 1735, at the age of 32, John Wesley boarded the good ship *Simmonds* and sailed off to the new world as an Anglican missionary to the colony of Georgia. But Wesley made no bones about his main reason for exchanging the comforts of England for the rigors of the frontier. He said, "My chief motive, to which all the rest is subordinate is the hope of saving my own soul."[2]

Wesley went to Georgia to minister to the "noble savages." But before long he discovered them to be less than noble. Rather, they were, in his words, "gluttons, drunkards, thieves, liars and murderers."

Finally, after two short years, he abandoned that mission in abject despair and returned to England a defeated, beaten, disillusioned young man. When he docked in the British port, he entered the following note in his *Journal*:

> I left my native country, in order to teach the Georgian Indians the nature of Christianity. But what have I learned myself in the meantime? Why, what I the least of all suspected, that I, who went to America to convert others, was never myself converted to God.[3]

Salvation by Faith Alone

In Wesley's own words, his spiritual saga had been "a refined way of trusting to my own works." Then, in the gracious providence of God, a young man by the name of Peter Bohler happened across Wesley's path. Within a few weeks Bohler became a close friend of John Wesley and his brother Charles. And not long into that relationship Peter Bohler sensed the heaviness of John's heart and the weariness of his frustrated soul. So he shared with the Wesley brothers the one message they desperately needed and had apparently never heard—the good news of salvation in Christ by faith alone.

Bohler urged John to renounce his feverish attempts to please God by the many good works he was doing, the rules he was keeping, the rituals he was observing and the laws he was obeying. He demonstrated how John's ceaseless efforts to earn salvation by his own merits had led directly to the disillusionment that was defeating him. He exhorted him to turn away from his do-it-yourself religion and trust

Christ's finished work on the cross as the sole source of his salvation.

It took many long discussions between these new friends. But finally, after many weeks of pondering this "new" message, John Wesley committed himself and all of his hopes for eternal salvation to the Christ who died for him. And in the famous heart-warming experience on Aldersgate Street, London, May 24, 1738, he came to Jesus and received the rest He offers. Immediately he was released from the weariness and exhaustion his do-it-yourself religion had thrust upon him.

John Wesley went on to live one of the most active, most involved, most influential lives ever recorded in history. Yet in all of his years of tireless devotion to Christ, never again did he grow weary in well-doing. Why? Because he experienced the constant refreshment that comes from the rest Christ offers.

Christ's Gift of Rest

There is a rest for the spirit that can be experienced only by coming to Jesus in repentance and faith and simply receiving it. If you sense that your soul is weary and your spirit soggy, your fatigue could stem from the overwhelming burden of a do-it-yourself religion. Whenever the Bible discusses the causes of spiritual weariness, it usually begins with legalism and its works-righteousness approach to salvation. Therefore, this is the place we must all begin in the diagnosis of what ails us.

Have you ever received the rest Jesus offers those who come to Him in honest-to-goodness repentance and faith? Have you ever placed all of your hope for eternal salvation in what Christ has done for you on the cross? Or are you relying even partially on the works you do, the rules you keep, the moral life you lead, the rituals you observe or the laws you obey?

If there is even the slightest tinge of self-help in your salvation, you are the very person Jesus is inviting to Himself in Matthew 11:28. He is calling all who are weary and exhausted by the oppressive burden of their do-it-yourself religion. We become unbearably weary in well-doing when we pursue salvation on our own merits rather than trusting ourselves completely to Christ. Do you enjoy the assurance that, beyond the shadow of a doubt, you are trusting Christ alone for your eternal destiny? If you are not certain of this, then your lack of His rest is the primary cause of your spiritual fatigue.

For five years prior to his conversion, Charles Hadden Spurgeon was an adolescent in great distress. Referring to the burden that overwhelmed his conscience in those dark years, Spurgeon writes, "It was my sad lot to feel the greatness of my sin without a discovery of the greatness of God's mercy."[4]

He tried desperately to please God by being good enough to deserve salvation. But his many failures made him painfully aware that he was not measuring up to God's expectations. Then it happened! On Sunday, January 6, 1850, at the age of 15, Spurgeon rose early to attend church in the village of Colchester. He was visiting friends in that village and his mother had asked him to attend a particular church. But a January blizzard descended on Colchester, and being unfamiliar with the community, Spurgeon was unable to find his way.

In the fury of the storm he stumbled down a side street and happened upon a tiny Methodist church. Feeling the need for shelter and warmth he entered and sat down under the balcony near the back. There were only 15 worshipers in the congregation that morning. Even the guest speaker had been unable to make it through the storm. Consequently, an unlettered man who, as Spurgeon remembered, could hardly read the Scriptures, entered the pulpit, announced his text, and read, "Look unto me, and be ye saved, all the ends of the earth" (Isa. 45:22, *KJV*).

In stark simplicity that uneducated, unprepared speaker began to show those 15 worshipers what it means to look unto Christ and be saved. At the apex of his message, he looked back under the balcony, fixed his compassionate eyes on young Spurgeon and said, "Young man, you are very miserable."

Thinking back on that startling experience, Spurgeon said, "So I was, but I had not been accustomed to being addressed in that way."

The preacher continued, "Ah, and you will always be miserable, if you don't do as my text tells you; and that is, look unto Christ."[5]

Charles Spurgeon did just that. In that out-of-the-way place, a nowhere on the map, he came to Christ in repentance and faith. He renounced his reliance on his own efforts and looked to Jesus as the sole source of his salvation. And as he did, he received Christ's gift of rest for his weary soul. At once his burden of frustration and guilt was lifted and he went on his way to become one of the most liberated leaders of the church of his day.

The weariest people in all the world are those who

are overwhelmed by the burden of their do-it-your-self religion. Are you one of them? You can receive rest for your spirit and relief from your troubled conscience if you will respond to Christ's invitation: "Come to me, all who labor and are heavy laden, and I will give you rest."

Notes

1. Emma Lazarus, "The New Colossus," 1883.
2. John Wesley, *Letters*, vol. 1, p. 188. Quoted by A. Skevington Wood, *The Burning Heart* (Grand Rapids: Wm. B. Eerdmans Publishing Co., 1967), p. 51.
3. John Wesley, *Journal*, vol. 1, p. 422. Quoted by Wood, *The Burning Heart*, p. 57.
4. Charles Haddon Spurgeon. Quoted by Ernest Bacon, *Spurgeon, Heir of the Puritans* (Grand Rapids: Wm. B. Eerdmans Publishing Co., 1968), p. 20.
5. Bacon, *Spurgeon*, p. 23.

3
SOMETHING BETTER THAN GERITOL

Come to me, all who labor and are heavy laden, and I will give you rest. Take my yoke upon you, and learn from me; for I am gentle and lowly in heart, and you will find rest for your souls. For my yoke is easy, and my burden is light (Matt. 11:28-30).

A secular book that has touched me deeply is *Working*.[1] It is an eloquent exposé of people's feelings about their jobs. In the book people talk about their daily humiliations and frustrations in the humdrum monotony of their work. They speak of their search for meaning as well as for bread, their desire for recognition as well as for cash, and their quest for life in their Monday-to-Friday kind of death. You do not have to listen below the surface to pick up the vibrations of the average person's hunger for beauty, for meaning, for a sense of pride in what he does, for a feeling of accomplishment, for the satisfaction that he is making a vital contribution to life by what he does for a living.

These people who hunger for fulfillment in their work are in the office as well as the warehouse, at the manager's desk as well as the assembly line, in the executive suite as well as the kitchen. You cannot read *Working* without being gripped by the awareness that there is more than a slight ache in the heart of the American worker. There is the auto worker who "teases one guy 'cause he's real short and his old lady left him." And when he is asked "Why?" he replies, "Oh, just to break the monotony. You want quittin' time so bad."[2]

Mike LeFevre, a steelworker from Cicero, Illinois summed it up well when he said, "It isn't that the average working guy is dumb. He's tired, that's all."[3]

He is tired of work that does not satisfy his hunger for beauty, for meaning, for fulfillment, for the joy that comes from knowing he is making a vital contribution to life.

It was to people like these Jesus said: "Come to me, all who labor and are heavy laden, and I will give you rest. Take my yoke upon you, and learn from me; for I am gentle and lowly in heart, and you will find rest for your souls. For my yoke is easy, and my burden is light."

Those verses contain two key words—*yoke* and *rest*. Both words are used twice and neither can stand alone. They are inseparably linked one to the other. The implication of Christ's invitation is obvious. Without taking His yoke upon us we will never find emotional, psychological and/or spiritual rest. And when we take His yoke upon us we must find rest. Weariness that ends in despair, and fatigue that follows frustration do not find their source in the Saviour. His yoke brings rest to everyone who wears it.

Yokes Can Choke or Stroke

The word *yoke* was a familiar word to Christ's contemporaries. A yoke was what they placed on a beast of burden to bind him to an implement he was to pull, a plow, a sled, a wagon or whatever. Because the yoke bound the beast to its burden, Jesus used the word as a metaphor for "slavery," "bondage." He implied in His invitation that everyone has a yoke. All of us are enslaved in some form of bondage. All of us are yoked to something or someone.

Some are yoked to legalism in a frantic pursuit of do-it-yourself religion. Others are slaves to license in an equally frantic pursuit of pleasure, not because they want to, but because they have to. But most of us are yoked to the mundane cares of life in pursuit of beauty, meaning, fulfillment, happiness and a sense of well-being. And the object of Christ's invitation is to motivate us to exchange our yoke for His. He says, "Take my yoke upon you, and learn from me. Take off your present yoke, lay it down and take mine instead."

Now, what difference does it make whether I carry my present yoke or Christ's? One life of servitude is the same as another. Is it? This is the point where Jesus begs to differ with us. For He claims that His yoke is distinctively different from any other yoke known to man. His yoke is radically revolutionary. What makes it so revolutionary is that it brings rest and relief to the wearer, not weariness, oppression and the tiredness of which Mike LeFevre spoke.

"Take my yoke upon you, and learn from me, for

I am gentle and lowly in heart, and you will find rest for your souls." What a radical statement! Jesus claims that we can find freedom in bondage. We can find rest in slavery. We can experience relief while saddled with a yoke! But, the yoke must be His! The bondage must be to His will for us. The slavery must be total submission to Him. Being yoked to anything or anyone else leads only to frustration and fatigue, weariness and despair.

Earl Palmer tells of a sailor in the ancient world who was yoked to the goddess Diana. Everywhere he sailed he took that 45-pound bronze beauty along. Unfortunately one day he fell overboard. But, fortunately he held onto his idol and she fell overboard with him. There he was in the middle of the Mediterranean rubbing her head and trying to remember the incantations that would motivate Diana to rescue him. He was treading water furiously, trying to keep himself afloat while he recited the incantation. But Diana proved no help to him. In fact, her 45 pounds became an unbearable drag. And as he lost energy, he realized he had two options. Either he could jettison his idol and look for some other source of help or he could hang onto his idol and let it take him to the bottom.[4]

Does that sound farfetched to you? It shouldn't. That drama is played out on the stage of this world in millions of lives every day. People discover they are yoked to an idol that has become a drag. It brings them no beauty, no meaning, no fulfillment, no satisfaction, no salvation from the chaos and dreariness of life. And it suddenly occurs to them that they must either jettison that yoke and look for another source of help, or their idol will take them to the bottom. To all who have reached that crossroads, Jesus says, "My yoke is different. It brings rest, not weariness. It offers relief, not fatigue. It is freedom, never a drag."

Christ's Yoke Is Tailor-Made

Why does Christ's yoke bring rest and relief to the wearer when every other yoke of life brings oppression, weariness and frustrating fatigue? Because Christ's yoke is tailor-made to the wearer's uniqueness. When Jesus claims His "yoke is easy," He does not mean it involves no cost or requires no price from the one who wears it. He lays heavy demands on everyone who is willing to submit to His authority and wear His yoke. Many have been martyred because they wore the yoke of Christ. Therefore, His yoke is not easy in the sense that the wearer pays no price for wearing it. To submit to the yoke of Christ and to let Him call the shots in your life can be a very costly experience. *Easy* literally means "well-fitting, suitable, tailor-made."

In Palestine, ox-yokes were made of wood. The ox was brought to a carpenter's shop where its measurements were taken. Then the yoke was roughed out, the ox was brought back and the yoke was then carefully adjusted for perfect fit. It was tailor-made to suit the animal's individual measurements so it would not irk, chafe or gall the ox in any way. In this invitation Jesus draws upon the imagery of the carpenter shop that He knew so well. Many were the yokes He had made for the burden-bearing beasts. Now He is applying the same metaphor to people.

31

Jesus claims that all who take His yoke of authority upon them will find rest and relief. And the reason why His yoke is restful and not oppressive is because it is tailor-made to fit the unique measurements of each person who wears it. All other yokes chafe, irk and gall their wearers with weariness, frustration, fatigue and oppression because they don't fit. They aren't suited to their uniqueness. They aren't tailor-made for their distinctive individuality. Only Christ makes a yoke that really fits well. Therefore, only His yoke brings rest and relief to the wearer.

Dr. Louis Evans, Sr. tells of a visit to a mission station in Korea. A medical missionary friend invited him to witness an operation involving major surgery in a makeshift tent out in the sticks. The heat was stifling. The odors were oppressive. Hour after hour the steady, calm, determined surgeon worked on an old peasant woman. Finally, after seven hours, the doctor stepped back, lifted his mask and sighed, "Well, the job is done, Lou."

Together they returned to the missionary's modest office where Dr. Evans asked, "I'm curious, how much do you get paid out here in Korea for an operation like this?" The surgeon replied, "To begin with, I get this," and he held up a dented copper coin. "This poor old woman came in here some time ago with this old coin and said, 'Doctor, do you suppose this would pay for the operation?' I answered, 'It so happens that it is just enough.' So to begin with I get this piece of change."

Sitting down, with a warm moisture filling his learned eyes, the dedicated surgeon continued, "But most of all, Lou, what I get is the wonderful feeling that for seven hours Christ is living in these ten fingers! I have the priceless awareness that these hands become the hands of Jesus Christ healing one of His children."[5]

There is a man who has found rest under the yoke of Christ. He has found that the yoke Christ has laid upon his life is tailor-made to his uniqueness. He answered the call of Christ, submitted to the authority of Christ and discovered to his delight that the very thing Jesus commissioned him to do is the thing that brings him the deepest joy and the greatest sense of fulfillment. So it is with everyone who submits to the yoke of Christ.

When you lay down your idols, come to Christ, take His yoke upon you, begin to submit to His authority, do His will, run His errands and yield your life to His control, you will get tired at times, even as this surgeon in Korea was exhausted after that seven hour ordeal. But your tiredness, like his, will be filled with the joy of a job well done. Even in the midst of your exhaustion there will be the satisfying awareness that God has used you to do something worthwhile. He has enabled you to make a vital contribution to life.

That experience of fulfillment, more than anything else, is what brings rest to your soul. It is the kind of feeling that the Mike LeFevres and all other weary souls in this world have never experienced—the sense of joy, of beauty, of meaning and of fulfillment that this surgeon knows. Why haven't they experienced that kind of rest? Because they are wearing a yoke that doesn't fit. Only Christ makes a yoke that brings rest to the wearer.

Are you weary in well-doing? Are you frustrated with your yoke and fatigued by the lack of beauty and meaning and satisfaction you find in the obligations you face? If so, then you can be sure you are not yoked to Christ. Because His yoke brings rest. Bondage to His will generates relief from weariness. Running His errands will make you tired, to be sure. But it will be a wholesome tiredness, a welcome exhaustion that will give you time to recharge your batteries. And there will be, in that tiredness, the refreshing awareness that Jesus has used you to do something vital for His glory. That awareness will bring a beautiful sense of rest to your soul. The first reason why Christ's yoke brings rest to the wearer is because it fits so well. It is tailor-made to the unique measurements of each person who submits to it. Thus the wearing of that yoke brings joy and beauty, meaning and fulfillment, not fatigue and frustration, weariness and despair.

Christ's Yoke Binds Him to You

The yoke that Christ lays upon everyone who submits to His authority is a yoke of love. His yoke binds us to a Person, not a burden. And that Person is Jesus Christ, Himself.

There is a familiar old story of a man who came upon a little boy carrying upon his back a still smaller boy who was lame.

"That's a heavy burden for you, little boy," said the man.

"That's not a burden," came the answer. "That's my brother."

The burden which is given in love and borne in love

is always light. That is what Jesus means when He says, "My burden is light."

The word *light* means "insignificant." In other words Jesus claims that His yoke is insignificant to the wearer. It won't weigh you down or weary you. It is like wings to a bird and fins to a fish. Why? Because that very yoke is the source of your power. It not only binds you to Christ, it binds Him to you. And with Him comes His power that enables you to function without fatigue.

What would you think if I lifted up the hood of your car, pointed to your motor and asked, "Why do you carry this big chunk of iron around with you? Look at all the weight it adds to your automobile! How much easier this car would be to push if you did not have this heavy motor here in the front!"[6]

You would look at me in pity and shock and say, "My dear friend, you do not understand! It is the weight of that pile of metal that makes the difference between pushing and riding. The motor is what lets me ride. Without it I must push. So who cares how much the motor weighs?"

So it is with the yoke of Christ. That yoke is the source of His power in your life. It makes the difference between huffing and puffing and pushing through life, or riding under His power. His yoke binds Him to you as much as you to Him and that is what makes His yoke such an experience of rest and relief. His yoke becomes your source of strength, your inlet of power.

Christ's Yoke Brings Freedom

As you submit to Christ's demands upon your life,

surrender to His control and yield to His will, you discover the beautiful surprise that you don't lose freedom, you gain freedom. You don't lose control, you gain control. You don't lose yourself, you gain Christ.

When I think of someone who is yoked to Christ and Christ to her I think of Ann Kiemel.[7] To read the scintillating anecdotes of her life in her books is to see the difference between pushing and riding. Whether she is talking to a disheartened cab driver in Miami, taking her paperboy fishing, sending flowers to a lonely friend, or baking cookies for the new young couple in the apartment building, there is the refreshing evidence of Christ's yoke tailored to the unique style of her life. His yoke energizes her every moment with the power that makes the difference.

Are you pushing or riding? Are you huffing and puffing through the motions of your duties, frustrated with fatigue and weary with the burden of it all? Are you a candidate for Geritol? If you are, my friend, it is because you are not wearing the yoke of Christ. For, His yoke is not burdensome. It does not weary the wearer with fatigue and frustration. It will not chafe, irk or gall. Rather it fulfills the wearer with a sense of purpose and a source of power.

George Matheson said it all in the words of his famous prayer:

> Make me a captive, Lord,
>   And then I shall be free:
> Force me to render up my sword,
>   And I shall conqueror be.
> I sink in life's alarms
>   When by myself I stand;

Imprison me within Thine arms,
   And strong shall be my hand.[8]
Will you lay down your yoke and take His? It will
mean the difference between rest and fatigue, relief
and weariness, riding and pushing.

Notes

1. Studs Terkel, *Working* (New York: Avon Books, 1972).
2. Terkel, *Working*, p. xviii.
3. Terkel, *Working*, p. 5.
4. Quoted by David Roper in the message, "Defilement that Delays" (Palo Alto, Calif.: Discovery Publishing), p. 3.
5. Robert Schuller, *Self-Love* (Old Tappan, N.J.: Fleming H. Revell Co., 1975), pp. 32,33.
6. Ray Stedman in the message, "Christians Unabridged" (Palo Alto, Calif.: Discovery Publishing), p. 5.
7. Ann Kiemel, *I'm Out to Change My World* (Nashville: Impact Books, 1974), and *I Love the Word Impossible* (Wheaton: Tyndale House Publishers, 1976).
8. George Matheson, "Christ's Bondservant."

4
LIVING WITH YOUR LIMITATIONS

I must boast; there is nothing to be gained by it, but I will go on to visions and revelations of the Lord. I know a man in Christ who fourteen years ago was caught up to the third heaven—whether in the body or out of the body I do not know, God knows. And I know that this man was caught up into Paradise—whether in the body or out of the body I do not know, God knows—and he heard things that cannot be told, which man may not utter. On behalf of this man I will boast, but on my own behalf I will not boast, except of my weaknesses. Though if I wish to boast, I shall not be a fool, for I shall be speaking the truth. But I refrain from it, so that no one may think more of me than he sees in me or hears from me. And to keep me from being too elated by the abundance of revelations, a thorn was given me in the flesh, a messenger of Satan, to harass me, to keep me from being too elated. Three times I besought the Lord about this, that it should leave me; but he said to me, "My grace is sufficient for you, for my power is made perfect in weakness." I will all the more gladly boast of my weaknesses, that the power of Christ may rest upon me. For the sake of Christ, then, I am content with weaknesses, insults, hardships, persecutions, and calamities; for when I am weak, then I am strong (2 Cor. 12:1-10).

What a preposterous story! It is faintly reminiscent of tales people tell about little green men and their flying saucers. It sounds more like science fiction than the Bible. Yet here it is in bold print. The apostle Paul claims he knows a man who was caught up to heaven without a spaceship, heard sounds and saw sights that cannot be described, lived to tell about it, and was returned to earth to resume life as before. Then he qualifies his story by admitting he isn't certain whether the man actually took the trip bodily or merely saw a vision. But regardless, the experience was powerfully real. So real, in fact, that though it happened 14 years previously, that man still lived with both the joyful memories and the painful consequences of that experience.

Then modestly, Paul admits he was the person in question. Due to the persistent persecution to which Paul was subjected as an aggressive spokesman for Jesus Christ, the question of his endurance became a matter of utmost importance. Therefore, in order to motivate Paul to endure his suffering and persist in his proclamation of the good news about Jesus, God gave him a preview of the glory he would share in the next life. Then, to keep Paul from becoming a "big head" about his extraordinary experience, God sent him a "thorn in the flesh."

God-Given Limitations

Exactly what Paul's "thorn in the flesh" was we cannot be sure. Many theories have been advanced. Obviously this "thorn in the flesh" was not something sinful. It was something of which God approved. Suffice it to say, it was a God-given limitation in Paul's life. It was a painful perimeter around his pride, a continual clamp upon his conceit, a tight rein on his vanity. It was a limitation God placed on Paul's life to keep him from becoming conceited.

How did Paul respond to this "thorn"? Not very well at first. He pled earnestly with God to remove it and to set him free from its harassment. But the Lord said, "No, Paul. I am not going to remove this limitation from your life. Rather, I want you to discover in this experience that My grace is all you need. I want you to learn that My power comes to its full strength at the point of your weakness." (See 2 Cor. 12:9.)

In other words, the Lord was trying to teach Paul that His power would make itself most evident when Paul was willing to acknowledge this limiting weakness, accept it, feel it and live with it. He was to stop begging for its removal and to start discovering the power God would give him at the point of that weakness, in the face of that frustrating limitation. Paul concludes this paragraph by telling us he was learning to live with this limitation. And though it was painful he was enjoying it, not because he was a masochist, but because it was a constant reminder of his weakness. And when he was fully conscious of his weaknesses—his God-given limitations—then God's power flowed through him freely and effectively.

One of the fundamental causes of emotional and spiritual fatigue among Christians is our refusal to live within the limitations God has laid upon our lives. Much of our weariness stems from our efforts to transcend those limitations, to throw them off and exchange them for someone else's strengths. When we engage in that struggle we become unbearably weary because we are rejecting the custom-made blueprint God designed for our lives. God says, "My grace is all you need, for My power comes to its full strength precisely at those points in your life where you know you are weak. So don't try to transcend them. Don't attempt to throw them off. Don't seek to exchange your thorns for someone else's roses. Accept the limits I have laid upon you. Feel them. Know them. Live with them. And you will discover that those limitations are the very points where my power expresses itself most effectively in your life."

We Are Limited by Our Humanity

In chapter 1, I shared with you my painful memories of an experience of depression that really laid me low. When, on the brink of despair, I spent the better part of an afternoon in prayer, pouring my heart, my anger, my self-pity and my frustrations out to God. And out of that experience there came some fresh insights from God. One crucial truth He taught me that afternoon is so basic, so fundamental, so elementary that I hesitate even to mention it.

In that time on my knees, the Lord reminded me that I am not God. Now, others knew that all along. But sometimes I forget. And in my forgetfulness I try to play God. I struggle to control things that are out of my control. I try to manage things I have no business managing. And in the process I succeed only in frustrating myself with fatigue and burdening myself with the blues.

I am consumed by a vision for the ministry of the church I pastor. Therefore, I am vulnerable to anything that looks like a serious threat to that vision. That is why I capsized as our people's financial response did not match my expectations. But in that experience, God really got through to me. He reminded me of the words of Jesus, "I will build my church, and the power of hell will not withstand it" (see Matt. 16:18).

Jesus claims it is His job to build His church. "I will build my church," says Jesus. God showed me in those dark days that here is where I was going wrong. I was playing Jesus. I was attempting to build His church. But Jesus backed me into a corner where He could show me that I had taken upon my shoulders a burden that was far too big for me to bear. I was trying to transcend the limits of my humanity and do what only God could do. Therefore, I was depressed, discouraged and weary to the point of despair.

It is Christ's responsibility to build His church, not mine. He designs the scheme by which He wants it to grow and thrive. It is my responsibility to be faithful, to catch the gleam of His scheme, to translate that scheme into a dream we can grasp and pursue, to recruit the team that can lead us in our quest of that dream, and to keep the team and the dream on His beam. That is the job He has given me. But His job is to design the scheme and then glean the harvest. Every time I forget that, and take His responsibilities on my shoulders, I become burdened with the blues, fatigued with frustration. Why? Because in assuming His responsibilities, I am rejecting the limitations of my humanity. And that always leads to weariness.

You are not much different from me in this respect. Do you ever worry? Worrying is nothing less than an attempt to transcend the limits of your humanity. It is an effort to control things that are beyond your control. It is a struggle to manage things you have no business managing.

Worry is public enemy number one. During World War II more than 300,000 of America's finest young men were killed in combat. During the same period over a million civilians died from heart disease, primarily caused by worry.[1]

Worry will break you if you persist in it. The tension that comes from man's unwillingness to live within the limitations of his humanity is the number one killer at large in the world today.

If you are stalked by this killer, I recommend you do what I did. Get alone with God and tell Him what's bugging you. Confess your worry. Admit that you have taken His responsibilities upon your shoulders. Tell Him that you want to give that burden back to Him. Ask Him to give you total freedom from it. And if you will, He will. He will take control of the thing you have been trying to control with your worrying. And, in exchange, He will give you His peace. It is peace that comes only when you are willing to accept the limitations of your humanity and live with them.

Five minutes after you give Him your worry, you may find yourself in a stew about the same issue again—you have taken back the burden you gave God. So, you must return it to Him again. And you must repeat that act of surrender as many times in a day as is necessary to be rid of your worry. You must learn to live with the limitations of your humanity. If you refuse, you court the number one killer. If you do it you will experience the fresh invasion of God's peace and power at the point of your weakness.

We Are Limited by Our Individual Uniqueness

We know that each of us is unique. We know that each of us is an unrepeatable miracle from the hand of God. When He made each of us, He threw away the mold. No two persons on the face of the earth have the same fingerprints or life-print. Each of us has been given a different combination of talents, gifts, abilities, energy and drive. We know all that. Yet many of us refuse to accept the particular combination we have been given. We look upon the limitations of our unique individuality as a thorn, and we envy someone else's rose. We reject our individual limitations and long to exchange them for someone else's package.

Fifteen years ago when I was attending college in the Chicago area, my hero was the pastor of a famous church in Chicago. Every Sunday I could, I worshiped with that congregation and sat under the ministry of that great man. And what an unparalleled privilege that was. Every week I would be inspired by his enthusiasm, moved by his oratory and gripped by his exposition of the Scriptures.

I remember on one occasion how he remonstrated us for sleeping one-third of our life away. There was much too much work for Christ to be done to spend eight hours out of every 24 in the sack. He exhorted us to discipline ourselves to function on six. So I tried. And I failed miserably.

Then, a few years later, I heard the sad news that this magnificent servant of God had suffered a massive cerebral hemorrhage. The apparent cause: overwork. He was driving himself beyond the limits of his uniqueness. Sometime later he confessed that his hero was the great A.W. Tozer, another famous pastor of that era. Tozer could thrive on four or five hours sleep a night. The man whom I admired told how he loved to meet Tozer in one of Chicago's parks in the early hours of the morning. And there the two or them would pray and share the Scriptures together. But while Tozer could live comfortably with that schedule, apparently this man could not. His attempt to stretch himself into Tozer's mold eventually broke him. And today he is but a shaking, emotionally-broken shadow of the man he once was.

Hardly a week passes that I do not encounter someone whose basic personal problem is a rejection of his self. Many of us just do not like living with ourselves. We despise the limitations of our heredity, the environment of our youth, our appearance, our build, our talent and the energy-quotient God has laid upon our life. We reject those limits. Our conversation betrays us. Our defenses give us away. We just don't like the limits God has built into our life.

Recently I participated in a pastors' conference in Chicago. There I was exposed to some of the superstars in the evangelical church of our generation. Edward Hill, renowned pastor of a thriving black congregation in Los Angeles, was there. Don Williams was there. His street ministry among freaks and straights of the 1960s youth culture in Hollywood is a legend on the West Coast. Myron Augsburger was there. His exceptional ability to think, write and preach are evident to anyone who has heard him. And Paul Rees was there.

As I sat under the ministry of those outstanding servants of God, I was confronted with a choice. Either I could compare my limitations to their apparent lack of limitations, my weaknesses to their strengths, my abilities to their exceptional abilities, and leave that conference picking at their flaws and crushed by my smallness; or I could open myself to God's Word to me through them and relish every minute of it, realizing all the while that, though I live to be 100, I will never be able to preach like Edward Hill. Nor will I be able to relate to people like Don Williams, nor write and speak like Myron Augsburger or Paul Rees. Realizing that, I could enjoy it all simply because God's great love gives me the ability to love me as I am and them as they are, and to dispense with all comparisons.

This does not mean that I must renounce all efforts to grow and stretch and become as effective as I can possibly become. Never! What it means is that I must not renounce the limitations God has implanted in my unique personality. I must grow and stretch and reach. But I must do it within the limits of my uniqueness. In other words, I must become the best possible me I can become by the grace of God flowing through me.

Living with Our Limitations

One of the fundamental causes of emotional and spiritual fatigue is our unwillingness to live with our limitations.

The cover story of an issue of *Campus Life* featured two girls by the same first name who attend the same high school, Laura Cheney and Laura Nash. The story focuses on the hatred the one Laura had for the other. Laura Nash was attractive, slim, petite and dressed like a model out of *Seventeen*. She was everything Laura Cheney wanted to be. And she hated her for it. Laura Cheney was 25 pounds overweight and viewed herself as unattractive and undesirable. Oh how miserable she was in her self-hatred! She despised everything about herself. She rejected her limitations and retreated into an inner world of "the blues."

Then two things happened to change all that. She attended a conference where she came face to face with the Christ who loved her just as she was. Opening her life to Christ's love she began to discover a desire to love and accept herself.

She returned home to become the best Laura Cheney she could possibly become. She enrolled in Weight Watchers and over the span of many months lost a bundle of pounds. Then, since Christ had given her the ability to accept the limitations of her individuality and even to like them, she was freed from her envy of the other Laura. She confessed her envy to God. Then she sought out the other Laura and confessed her envy to her.

As a result, Laura Cheney was surprised by two beautiful consequences. First, she was freed from her burden of the blues. Second, she made three dynamic friends: Jesus, herself and the other Laura.[2]

Like Paul with his thorn in the flesh, you may want to be freed from the limitations God has built into your life. You long to throw them off, to transcend them, to exchange them for someone else's strengths. And that struggle against your limitations, as much as anything else, is souring you with the blues. Will you listen to the Lord's Word to Paul, and make it yours? God says;

> My grace is all you need. For, my power comes to its full strength precisely at those points in your life where you know you are weak. So don't try to transcend them. Don't attempt to throw them off. Don't seek to exchange your thorns for someone else's roses. Accept the limits I have laid upon you. Feel them. Know them. Live with them. And you will discover that those limitations are the very areas where my power expresses itself most effectively in your life.

Notes

1. Mack Douglas, *How to Make a Habit of Succeeding* (Grand Rapids: Zondervan Publishing House, 1966), p. 77.
2. Laura Cheney and Laura Nash, "Two Lauras," *Campus Life*, (February, 1976), pp. 50-53.

5
SQUEAKING WHEELS AND BOWED KNEES

And in the morning, a great while before day, he rose and went out to a lonely place, and there he prayed. And Simon and those who were with him followed him, and they found him and said to him, "Everyone is searching for you." And he said to them, "Let us go on to the next towns, that I may preach there also; for that is why I came out." And he went throughout all Galilee, preaching in their synagogues and casting out demons (Mark 1:35-39).

Bruce Larson and Ralph Osborne tell of a businessman who taught them a vital lesson about life. They were meeting with the man in his office. And though the telephone rang intermittently, to their surprise he made no effort to answer it. Finally one of them asked him how he could resist answering the phone. He replied, "It is there for my convenience—not to tyrannize me. I could never do my job properly if I gave in to the demands of the telephone. If it's important for someone to get in touch with me, he knows he can write for an appointment."[1]

Admittedly, that is an extreme position to adopt toward the telephone or any other means of communication. Yet the man makes a point we need to grasp. Very few of us have discovered this kind of freedom from demanding distraction and incessant interruption. We live our days and nights victimized by the urgent and tyrannized by the peremptory demands life makes on our time, our energy and our attention. In other words, we live by the principle of the squeaking wheel.

The ancient proverb says, "The squeaking wheel gets the oil." So it is with life. Our society reflects this principle. Whatever minority happens to holler the hardest is the minority that gets the attention. In the 1960s, it was the blacks. And rightfully so. They were yesterday's squeaking wheel.

Today the women's movement is the current target for the oilcan. Tomorrow, who knows? Business reflects the principle of the squeaking wheel. The customer who complains the loudest usually gets the most catering. Our families live by the same principle. The child who gives his parents the most grief gets most of their time and energy.

So deeply is this principle woven into the warp and woof of our lives that we don't question its sovereignty. We submit to the demands of every squeak and whip our oilcan into action, never questioning whether this is the way God intends His people to live. Yet all the while, we realize that these squeaking wheels in our lives, in our families and in our environment at large are the very things causing much of the weariness we feel. We admit that our squeaking wheels propel us into perpetual motion.

So? What can we do about it? What alternative do we have? God calls us to responsibility as well as to freedom. How, then, can we be His responsible people in our families, on the job, at school, in our community without responding to the urgent needs, the immediate issues and the prevailing problems that press their demands upon us? Is there an alternative life-style to the perpetual motion of our present pattern? Yes, there is! That alternative to our perpetual motion is portrayed in the life of Jesus.

Even a casual study of the Gospels reveals how frequently Christ's ministry to people grew out of interruptions. And it is important to note how often Jesus transformed those interruptions into inspirations. But, having noted that vital dimension of His life and ministry, it is imperative to understand that Jesus never became enslaved by the spontaneous, tyrannized by the urgent or victimized by the immediate. He never lived by the principle of the squeaking wheel. His life was constantly invaded with incessant interruptions and peremptory demands. Yet, He never became the pawn of those pressures. Jesus remained free to say no to the urgent whenever the urgent would crowd out the ultimate.

The Father's Business Comes First

When Jesus was 12 He accompanied His earthly parents to the Passover Feast in Jerusalem—His first trip out of the hills of Nazareth to the big city of Jerusalem. For every Jew of that era, the chief attraction of Jerusalem was the Temple. And Jesus was no exception. In fact, He was so caught up in life at the Temple that when it came time for His family to leave for home, Jesus was not ready to leave.

His parents assumed He would respond to the urgent demands of their schedule and be in the crowd on the way to Nazareth with them. But when they checked, they discovered He was nowhere to be found. So, in genuine parental frenzy, they scurried back to Jerusalem, searched high and low and finally found Him where He had been all along—in the Temple. Mary and Joseph thrust on Jesus the typical parental guilt-inducer, "How could you do this to us? We expected you to respond to the immediate demands of the schedule just as we must! How could you be so irresponsible?" (see Luke 2:48).

Jesus replied with those wise, compassionate, wonderful words, "Did you not know that I must be about my Father's business?" (see Luke 2:49).

There is the first clue from the life of Jesus that though He would perform His ministry in a pressurecooker of peremptory demands and incessant interruptions, He would never allow the urgent to preempt the ultimate. He would never live by the principle of the squeaking wheel. Though His parents' schedule was important, it was more important for Him at that time to be intently engaged in a profound exchange of wisdom and truth with the doctors of the law and the teachers in the Temple. That was His Father's business for Him at that time and place.

The Primary Issue
In the opening chapter of Mark's Gospel, we wit-

ness another occasion when Jesus refused to let the urgent take precedence over the ultimate. Jesus had stolen away from His disciples in the early hours of the morning and had gone up into hills where He could converse with His heavenly Father in solitude. When Simon Peter awoke, he looked around for Jesus and could find Him nowhere. This disturbed Simon greatly because a huge crowd was gathering in the streets of Capernaum outside the house where Jesus and His disciples had stayed that night.

The previous day in Capernaum had been especially taxing on Jesus. Mark records the story of two amazing miracles Jesus had performed that day. Then Mark adds, "That evening, at sundown, they brought to him all who were sick or possessed with demons. And the whole city was gathered together about the door. And he healed many who were sick with various diseases, and cast out many demons" (Mark 1:32-34).

When evening came, Jesus dismissed the crowds and retired for the night. Now the sun returned with the light of a new day. And with it came the crowds in even greater number pressing about the door. But Jesus had beaten the crowds to the door and was off into the hills.

Simon couldn't understand that action. He sensed the strong pull of the crowd, the irresistible urge to perform for the people who had gathered for the performance. And the people were desperate. They had come with urgent needs, with painful hurts, with awful aches in their bodies, their souls and their spirits. So Simon and the other disciples went searching for Jesus. And when they found Him they exclaimed,

"Everyone is searching for you. They need you desperately. They want you! They love you!" (see Mark
1:37).

But Jesus shocked His disciples with this reply,
"Let us go on to the next towns, that I may preach
there also; for that is why I came out" (Mark 1:38).

That reply is shocking because it sounds again one
of the more shrill notes of Christ's ministry. Namely,
He would not allow the urgent to crowd out the ultimate. The needs in Capernaum were urgent to be
sure. There were many hurts to heal, many lives to
change, many souls to save, many troubles to transform. But Jesus refused to allow those pressing issues
to preempt the primary issue to which His Father was
calling Him. He knew that His Father's business for
the next several days was taking Him to other towns
of Galilee. So He left Capernaum and its urgent needs
behind, and went out to do the ultimate thing toward
which His Father was leading Him.

The Ultimate over the Urgent

The story of Christ's response to the news of Lazarus' illness is another illustration of His refusal to
yield to the urgent. His close friend Lazarus was dying. Everyone who knew how much Jesus loved
Lazarus and everyone who knew how much power
Jesus possessed expected Him to do the urgent thing
—to spare Lazarus from death. When Jesus failed to
meet their urgent demands, they became rather testy
with Him. But, Jesus was more concerned with the
ultimate than the urgent. The ultimate thing was to
raise Lazarus from death.

Why was that so important? John tells us it was the

one single event that precipitated the triumphal entry into Jerusalem on Palm Sunday. In other words, it introduced the final week of Christ's ministry prior to His crucifixion and resurrection. That is what the heavenly Father wanted at that time and place in His Son's ministry. He wanted Jesus on the cross, bearing our sins, dying in our place that we might live. That is why Jesus did not submit to the urgent demands of His friends to spare Lazarus from death.

The Gospels convince the reader that Jesus was tender, loving and compassionately responsive to the pains, hurts and cries of people around Him. But Jesus was never captured by His compassion, never enslaved by the spontaneous, never tyrannized by the urgent, and never victimized by the incessant interruptions that inundated Him.

Jesus refused to allow the urgent to take precedence over the ultimate. That is the reason, on the eve of His crucifixion, as He converses with His heavenly Father, He can say, "I glorified thee on earth, having accomplished the work which thou gavest me to do" (John 17:4).

How could Jesus claim He had accomplished the work His Father had given Him to do? Think of all the people whose hurts He didn't heal, whose problems He didn't solve, whose lives He didn't change, whose souls He didn't save, whose urgent needs He didn't meet, whose desperate cries He didn't answer. For every one He helped, a thousand with the same sores went without help. How then could Jesus have the nerve to tell His Father He had finished the work He had been assigned?

Here's how. Jesus knew the difference between the

urgent and the ultimate. And He would not let the one conflict with the other. Therefore, He refused to respond to the thing of urgent importance when that response would hinder Him from pursuing the thing of ultimate importance. He lived by a principle totally different from the squeaking wheel.

Discerning the Ultimate from the Urgent

As we bring this matter home to where you and I live, I think I can sense the question on the tip of your tongue. It's the how question, isn't it? You are talking to yourself, saying, "That's true! What you are saying is certainly true in my life. The squeaking wheels that call for my time, energy and attention are definitely the cause of my weariness. The people and things that bombard me with their incessant interruptions and their peremptory demands are the reasons for my fatigue.

"I am crowded by the urgent, crushed by the immediate and pressed into perpetual motion almost to the point of distraction. I am tired of my squeaking wheels. But what can I do? I would like to choose the ultimate over the urgent at least occasionally. I would like to opt for the important over the immediate, and the primary issue over the pressing issue. I would like my life to be characterized by faithfulness, not frenzy. But how? How can I know which is which? How can I be responsible and still be free? How can I come to the place in my life where I can say with Jesus, 'I am doing what you want me to do'?"

Here again Jesus provides the clue. He shows us how to live an exceedingly busy, pressure-packed, demanding life without growing weary in well-doing.

He provides the pattern that is responsible yet free, pressure-packed yet productive and peaceful.

What was His secret? It is really no secret at all. The Gospel writers make it too obvious to miss. They refer to this dimension of Jesus' life-style over and over again. What was it? How did Jesus know the difference between the urgent and the ultimate on that morning when Simon and his fellow disciples came running to Him with the tempting news, "Everyone is searching for you"? How did Jesus know that the time had come to ignore the urgent and pursue the ultimate?

The answer steps right out of the text. Jesus had an active prayer life! He had just spent several hours in conversation with His heavenly Father. That time of prayer filled Jesus with the settled conviction that His Father's business was taking Him elsewhere that day. Therefore, He had the freedom to walk away from that squeaking wheel totally without guilt or second thoughts.

You can practice the principle of the bowed knee. I do not recommend prayer as the solution to every problem. Prayer is not designed to be the all-encompassing panacea. But God lays many people and things on the doorstep of your life for which you are immediately responsible. Those people and things confront you constantly with their urgent needs, their peremptory demands and their incessant interruptions. They are your squeaking wheels. And they have propelled you into perpetual motion. So, with oilcan in hand, you run feverishly to meet their many demands. You are weary because you are living by the principle of the squeaking wheel.

But God doesn't want you to be weary. He wants to enable you to live by a totally different principle: the principle of the bowed knee. He wants you to be responsible to all of the wheels He rolls across your path. But He doesn't want you to be tyrannized by their every squeak.

To be victimized by the urgent demands life presses upon you is to grow weary. But to pray, to spend time alone and unhurried on your knees before God is to know the difference between the urgent and the ultimate. Prayer is the key that enables you to open the door to the important when you are being pressed by the immediate. Prayer was the single most important factor that enabled Jesus to be free in the midst of frenzy, to live a pressure-packed life without growing weary in well-doing.

Jesus learned to live by the principle of the bowed knee rather than the squeaking wheel. He established the pattern for us. If we want to be responsible yet free from the tyranny of our responsibility, we have no choice but to invest time in prayer. Sometimes the urgent is the avenue to the ultimate. Other times the urgent is the enemy of the ultimate. If we want to know when to give ourselves to the urgent, or when to ignore the urgent in favor of the ultimate, we must pray.

Prayer is the key to living a pressure-packed life without growing weary in well-doing. Why? Because in prayer, God shows us the difference between the urgent and the ultimate. He delivers us from perpetual motion and, instead, enables us to have a peaceful, productive life, faithful to Him and free from frenzy. And to be free from frenzy is to be free from fatigue.

You can be calm in chaos. On the evening of December 7, 1946, a businessman named Stuart Luhan checked into the Winecoff Hotel in Atlanta, Georgia. He requested and received a room on the tenth floor high above the city's traffic. Sometime after retiring, Mr. Luhan was awakened by commotion in the corridor. An ominous red glow reflected in the sky outside his window. Fire! Heart pounding with panic, he threw open his door into the corridor only to be engulfed by suffocating smoke. Retreating into his room he shut the door and the transom above, and ran to the window to fill his lungs with air. What he saw 10 stories below filled him with terror. For milling around fire trucks was a gathering crowd. Behind him he could hear the screams and cries of other residents on his floor.

Fear so consumed him that it pressed like a weight on his chest. But years before, Stuart Luhan had begun to cultivate the principle of the bowed knee. So he dropped to his knees and began to pray. As he communed with God in that unlikely setting, he began to change. Later he wrote:

> The first sure sign that God was with me in that fire-surrounded room was that after this prayer my fear just left me, siphoned off like poison. Judging from the sounds around me and the increasing heat in the room, the situation was getting worse by the minute. Yet on the inside was a center of calm, such calmness that I really could hear the inner voice.[2]

The first instruction was that he should put his clothes on. The next clear suggestion was to make a rope of the sheets, the blankets and even the bed-spread. As he secured the knot he realized his "rope" would not reach more than a few stories to the street. But he followed instructions, feeling certain he would be told what to do next.

When his rope was completed, he began lowering it out the window only to be stopped abruptly by the command of that inner Voice: "No—not yet, trust Me." How dumb, he thought. What more urgent, more important thing could anyone do in a burning building but get out as soon as he can, any way he can? So again he proceeded to throw the rope out the window. And again came the crisp order from within, "Not yet! Wait."

It took willpower and strong self-discipline to obey such a "questionable" command. For now black smoke was seeping into the room. Any delay seemed fatal. But years earlier, Mr. Luhan had learned to check signals with his Master and to submit to His strategy. So he waited. The minutes dragged like hours.

Finally came the word he longed to hear, "Now is the time. Put the rope out the window. Tie it around the center of the window frame and climb out." As Stuart Luhan climbed over the sill, he saw a fireman extending a ladder to the eighth floor—as far as it would reach. Even so it was still too far away, one room to the right.

Suddenly the fireman saw him hanging there. Through a series of death-defying "stunts" with rope and ladder, Stuart Luhan was able to swing over to the fireman's ladder and climb down to safety. The whole process took but a few moments. Yet, when he

60

planted his feet on "terra firma" and looked up to the perch from which he had swung, he realized why the voice had delayed his departure. For ten floors up, his improvised rope was withering in flames. Had he lowered the rope when he thought it to be so urgently wise to do, his rope would have been engulfed in flames from the side of the building before that fireman could rescue him. And he would have plummeted to his death.

That is a highly dramatic story, to be sure. Yet your life, lived under the tyranny and tension of your squeaking wheels is no less filled with the fear and frenzy Mr. Luhan felt in that burning building. That frenzy is largely responsible for your fatigue. Therefore, you need to be set free from the tyranny of your squeaking wheels. You can be if you will submit all of your wheels to Jesus and let Him enable you to live by His pattern—the principle of the bowed knee.

Notes

1. Bruce Larson and Ralph Osborne, *The Emerging Church* (Waco: Word Books, 1970), p. 15.
2. Catherine Marshall, *Beyond Ourselves*. Copyright © 1961 by Catherine Marshall. Used with permission of McGraw-Hill Book Company, pp. 137-139.

6
HANDLING YOUR HASSLES

Have this mind among yourselves, which you have in Christ Jesus, who, though he was in the form of God, did not count equality with God a thing to be grasped, but emptied himself, taking the form of a servant, being born in the likeness of men. And being found in human form he humbled himself and became obedient unto death, even death on a cross (Phil. 2:5-8).

During the fighting on the island of Okinawa in 1945, a brilliant and feisty marine from the slums of Manhattan was hit in the hand by a Japanese sniper's bullet. The bullet went through his wrist without breaking a bone, ricocheted off a bazooka shell he was carrying and lodged in his chest over his heart. This tough man of steel who had been fearless in combat, exposing himself to danger time after time in heroic manner, collapsed. Looking at the bullet barely sticking into his chest, he was convinced it had entered his heart and he fell over dead.

The doctors were amazed. A minor flesh wound,

not even a broken bone. They pulled the bullet out with tweezers. It had come nowhere near his heart. He died of fright.[1]

Human experiences like this demonstrate what a devastating effect our emotions can have on our lives. Unhealthy emotions can kill even the strongest and best of us. Therefore, it is easy to see why our destructive feelings are major contributors to the fatigue we feel and the weariness we fight. For example, people in the world of medicine tell us that five minutes of intensive hatred burns more energy than eight hours of strenuous work. Now, if you have unlimited energy, you can afford to indulge in some delicious hates. But most of us have only so much energy to spend. We have none to spare. Therefore, we must conserve it and concentrate it solely on the positive purposes God has called us to pursue.

But many of us fail to focus our energy only on God's positive purposes for us. Rather, we dissipate it on the resentments we relish, the hurts we harbor, the bitterness we brood in, the fears we feel, the frustrations we fondle, the aggravations we accumulate, the hatred we harvest and the anger we express, suppress or repress. And these unhealthy emotions foment our inner hassles, hassles that burn up our energy. Thus we lack sufficient reserve to live the life God wants us to live.

But there is a better way to live. Indeed, a new way. It is the way Jesus lived. Many glimpses of Jesus in the Gospels show Him to be a person of limited energy. His constitution did not embody endless reserves of strength. He knew what it meant to be fatigued after a demanding day. He became exhausted just as we do. He needed sleep and retreat from pressure.

Though Jesus was a person of limited energy, one of the great differences between Him and us lay in His use of that energy. He did not dissipate any of it on destructive emotions that foment inner hassles. On the contrary, He focused His energy singularly on the positive purposes God called Him to pursue.

Jesus shows us how to handle our hassles in a healthy way. Though He was incessantly surrounded by conflict and controversy, He did not allow those external conflicts to become internal hassles. In other words, He gave no room and no vent to destructive emotions. In this chapter and the next, I want to show you how Jesus handled His hassles. We will isolate three principles in His life, placard them before us and learn from Him how to handle our external conflicts before they become internal hassles. These principles are: *Jesus renounced His rights; Jesus renounced rigidity; Jesus renounced retreat.*

Renouncing Our Rights

To those who have profited from Bill Gothard's seminar on Basic Youth Conflicts, talk about yielding or renouncing our rights sounds familiar. I must confess how much I have benefited from Gothard's insight at this point. Hardly a week passes that I do not recognize new areas where this principle should be applied in my life.

Talk of renouncing one's rights is certainly unwelcome at a time in our history when we just celebrated the two-hundredth anniversary of our nation's revolution. Had it not been for our courageous forefathers who demanded their rights, we today would not be enjoying the right to life, liberty and the pursuit of happiness we cherish so highly. Therefore, the principle of renouncing one's rights is understandably unwelcome.

Likewise, talk of renouncing one's rights is unpopular in today's world of "assertiveness training" for women and others whose rights have been denied. A few months ago *The Minneapolis Star* featured a major article on assertiveness training for women under the heading, "Do You Stick Up for Your Rights?"[2] The article told of the many seminars springing up all across our country, training women how to know their rights, and how to fight for, assert and demand their rights. And like its political counterpart of 200 years ago, today's quest for women's rights has merit.

But life shows us that the struggle to assert our rights, be it on a national level, a neighborhood level or an individual level is not all it's cracked up to be. In fact, the fight to secure our rights and to get everything coming to us is known to be one of the major causes of emotional fatigue. The man spoke for many of us when he said, "I spend 75 percent of my time and energy doing my job and the other 25 percent making sure that someone else doesn't do me."[3]

By his own admission, that man's fear of being deprived of his rights dissipated 25 percent of his energy. No wonder he could not give 100 percent to the positive purposes God called him to pursue. Here's why it is so imperative for us to follow Christ's example and renounce our rights before the struggle to maintain them becomes an inner hassle we can't handle.

65

Both the Bible and life teach us that the struggle to secure our rights is tied inseparably to resentment, bitterness, anger, hatred and fear, the five destructive emotions that siphon off most of our energy. To assert our rights and demand everything that is coming to us is to thrust ourselves into a vicious vortex of resentment and its kissing cousins. For, what causes resentment, bitterness and the ensuing anger with its fear and its hatred? Are these destructive emotions not triggered primarily by some legitimate right that has been denied the offended party? But these destructive emotions dissipate our energy and frustrate us with fatigue. And they will eventually destroy us if we give continued room and vent to them. Therefore, we must find a way to rid ourselves of them continually.

A few minutes after I had finished writing this chapter, I left the office and drove home. As I made my way along the street, I was startled suddenly by a car hurtling toward me from a side street. Realizing the driver was not going to stop, I braked, and watched him sail across in front of me. Immediately, the man who had just written these words on "renouncing rights" became filled with a surge of destructive emotions. My strong awareness of the rights I had just been denied aroused sudden feelings of resentment, anger and fear. If only I had been driving a tank. Yet, what a childish, destructive way to respond to life.

Jesus Is Our Example
Jesus offers us a better way. He shows us that the first step on the road to handling our hassles is to

renounce our rights, to yield them to God and to let Him handle them. In the second chapter of Paul's letter to Christians at Philippi, he enumerates some of the rights Jesus was willing to renounce in order to be our Saviour.

First, Jesus renounced the right to be equal with His heavenly Father during His ministry on this earth. Jesus was God. Yet He set aside that right voluntarily and came into this world to assume our humanity and to identify with us in our hassles.

Second, Jesus renounced the right to be king. Though He was King of kings and Lord of lords—though He was the Creator of all that is—He renounced His right to enter this world as a king and came instead as a servant. He hailed from peasant stock back in the hills of insignificant Galilee, from a no-name place called Nazareth.

Third, Jesus renounced the right to call His own shots, to be His own boss, and do His own will. He voluntarily submitted to the will of His heavenly Father at every point. He became obedient to His Father.

Fourth, Jesus renounced His right to live. The Bible claims that the primary reason why we die is not old age or illness or accident. The fundamental cause of death among human beings is sin. We die because we are sinners. But Jesus was not a sinner. He was different, the only one to walk this earth without committing even one sin. Therefore, Jesus is the only one who deserved to live. Yet, the good news of the New Testament is that Jesus surrendered His right to live and willingly gave His life in the place of sinners like you and me.

The point is, you cannot touch a person like that with the embers of resentment, the coals of bitterness, the fires of hatred and anger or the goose bumps of fear. He was absolutely untouchable by these destructive emotions that create our inner hassles. Why? Because He renounced all His rights.

His enemies tried to stir up resentment and reaction in Jesus. They deprived Him of His right to privacy, His right to an honest hearing and His right to a fair trial. But that did not trouble Him. Why? Because He had renounced His rights to privacy and popularity and fair treatment.

They tried to paralyze Him with fear by marshaling their power, their prestige and their troops against Him. Yet, on the eve of His crucifixion, when they invaded the Garden of Gethsemane with spears and swords and a battalion of soldiers, He was totally unafraid and unimpressed by their awesome show of power. Why could they not hassle Jesus with fear? Because He had renounced even His right to live. And a person who has renounced his right to live is totally beyond the reach of the hassle of fear.

Alexandr Solzhenitsyn borrowed this page from the life of Jesus. And when he applied it to himself, it transformed his outlook on life. In the section of *The Gulag Archipelago* where he describes the awful methods used by Russian interrogators to force their political prisoners to confess, Solzhenitsyn turns to the question of endurance. He writes:

> So what is the answer? How can you stand your ground when you are weak and sensitive to pain, when people you love are still alive, when you are unprepared? What do

you need to make you stronger than the interrogator and the whole trap? From the moment you go to prison you must put your cozy past firmly behind you. At the very threshold, you must say to yourself: "My life is over, a little early to be sure, but there's nothing to be done about it. I shall never return to freedom. I am condemned to die—now or a little later . . . . I no longer have any property whatsoever. For me those I love have died, and for them I have died. From today on, my body is useless and alien to me. Only my spirit and my conscience remain precious and important to me."

Confronted by such a prisoner, the interrogation will tremble. Only the man who has renounced everything can win that victory.[4]

In those paragraphs Solzhenitsyn captures the secret that enabled Jesus and all who will follow Him to live beyond the reach of resentment, bitterness, fear and other inner hassles that dissipate energy and usher in weariness, weakness and collapse. A few pages later Solzhenitsyn tells of his own arrest and interrogation. He says:

Not only was I not in the least prepared to cut my cozy ties with earth, I was even quite angry for a long time because a hundred or so Faber pencils had been taken away from me when I was arrested.[5]

As long as he fumed and fussed about the loss of his rights—his rights to freedom as an innocent man, his rights to his family, his career and his pencils—he was like putty in the enemy's hands. For his resentment, bitterness, anger, hatred and fear over the loss of his rights made him terribly vulnerable to their brutality. But when he learned the lesson that Jesus lived, and began renouncing his rights to his pencils, to his career, to his freedom, to his family, yes, and even to life itself, then he became a tower of strength to himself, to his fellow prisoners and now to the world at large.

That is the life-style to which Jesus calls His followers. He says, "If any man would come after me, let him deny himself and take up his cross and follow me" (Mark 8:34).

A cross is something you die on. Therefore, to take up your cross means to renounce your right to live the kind of life you think you deserve to live. And contrary to what you might think, that is not a downer. It is an upper. It is the most liberating life-style any man, woman or child can pursue. It is liberating because it sets a person totally beyond the reach of resentment, bitterness, anger, fear and hatred—the major destructive emotions that create our inner hassles.

Therefore, if we would take the first step in handling our hassles, we must renounce our rights. To renounce our rights is the first step because it defuses the explosives in our destructive emotions.

The comic strip "B.C." has something to say to us. One of the characters, sitting in his fur loincloth, opens a box. A letter in the box says, "Congratulations! You have just purchased the world's finest fire-starting kit!"

The next scene shows him reading on.

The flint is of the finest stone imported from

the Orient. Your striker has been handcrafted by Old World craftsmen. The kindling has been carefully selected by screened lumberjacks. Your kit was packaged and inspected by little old grannies working in a dust-free environment and your fire kit dealer has sworn an oath of devotion to customers.

In the next picture he is back to his old methods, rubbing two sticks together. One of the cavewomen comes by and asks, "What's with the sticks? Where is your new fire-starting kit?" He looks up, smiles and says, "I built a shrine around it."

Jesus Is Our Enabler

Jesus shows us how He handled His hassles. And what do we do about it? We build a shrine around His example. But Jesus doesn't want us to do that. He is more than our example. He is also our enabler. It is true that He exemplified a life of peace in the midst of conflict.

Though Jesus was constantly surrounded by external conflict, He did not let those external conflicts become internal hassles for Him. Rather, He handled those potential hassles by renouncing His rights. Now, having learned that, it is easy for us to make the mistake the character in "B.C." made—to stand at a distance and admire Christ's example; indeed, to build a shrine around it. But Jesus doesn't want admirers. He wants followers.

Jesus wants to build His enabling power into us so that we will be able to handle our hassles as He handled His. Jesus said, 'Peace I leave with you; my peace I give to you; not as the world gives do I give to you. Let not your hearts be troubled, neither let them be afraid" (John 14:27).

In that promise Jesus affirms the truth that He will give us the very peace that enabled Him to live a life of wholeness in the midst of conflict. He doesn't promise to spare us from conflict. What He promises is that He will enable us to handle our external conflicts so they do not become internal hassles. In other words, He assures us that we can have the power to live beyond the reach of resentment, bitterness, anger, hatred and fear.

How to Handle Your Hassles

How can we have that power, the power that gives us inner peace in a pell-mell world? By doing what He did. He was God. Yet He renounced His right to be equal with God and became man. He was King of kings. Yet He renounced His right to be king over men and became a servant of men. He, of all people, had the right to run His own life. Yet He renounced His right to be His own boss and surrendered His will totally to the will of His heavenly Father. He of all people had the right to live. Yet He renounced that right and gave His life so that through His death we might live. And by renouncing His rights He was set free from the tyranny of every destructive emotion that could have created conflict within Him.

Jesus makes that very same option available to you and me. He calls us to follow Him. He promises His peace to all who do, His wholeness in the midst of conflict, His power to handle our hassles. He says, "If you would learn to handle your hassles and live by my peace, the first thing you must do is renounce your rights. Take up your cross and follow me. Re-nounce your rights to everything in life that you think you have coming to you—your property, your career, your privacy, your freedom, your family, your health, your sanity, yes, and even life itself. Renounce your right to it all. Yield those rights to me. And I will free you from the tyranny of the destructive emotions that are fomenting your hassles. I will enable you to handle your hassles. I will give you my peace. But, first, you must give me your rights."

Will you do that? All who do will take the first positive step in handling their hassles and thereby winning over weariness.

Postscript

While Jesus calls each of us to renounce our own rights and to surrender them to Him, He never asks us to renounce the rights of another. On the contrary, His followers are summoned into the forefront of the struggle to secure and maintain the rights of people whose rights have been denied. Hence the death-defying ministry of Corrie and Betsie ten Boom and all other courageous Christians who honor their Lord by involving themselves in the fight for other people's rights.

The difference between fighting for one's own rights and fighting for the rights of another lies in the difference between destructive and constructive emotions. When we give ourselves unselfishly to the struggle for another's welfare, we are using anger and hatred in a positive way. It is good to get angry enough at evil to do something constructive to defeat it. It is good to hate wickedness sufficiently to rise up in opposition against it, or, as Jesus did, to lay down one's life so that others can be freed from the tyranny of that wickedness. Jesus shows us that both anger and hatred can be constructive emotions when they are aroused and vented unselfishly on behalf of other people's rights.

Notes

1. Mack Douglas, *Success Can Be Yours* (Grand Rapids: Zondervan Publishing House, 1968), p. 103.
2. Judy Strick, "Do You Stick Up for Your Rights?" *The Minneapolis Star*, Friday, February 6, 1976, p. 1B.
3. Douglas, *Success*, p. 116.
4. Alexandr Solzhenitsyn, *The Gulag Archipelago* I and II (New York: Harper and Row Publishers, Inc., 1973), p. 130.
5. Solzhenitsyn, *Archipelago*, pp. 133, 134. Used by permission.

7
HANDLING
MORE OF YOUR
HASSLES

Again he entered the synagogue, and a man
was there who had a withered hand. And
they watched him, to see whether he would
heal him on the sabbath, so that they might
accuse him. And he said to the man who had
the withered hand, "Come here." And he
said to them, "Is it lawful on the sabbath to
do good or to do harm, to save life or to kill?"
But they were silent. And he looked around
at them with anger, grieved at their hardness
of heart, and said to the man, "Stretch out
your hand." He stretched it out, and his hand
was restored. The Pharisees went out, and
immediately held counsel with the Herodi-
ans against him, how to destroy him (Mark
3:1-6).

In the previous chapter we observed that our unresolved inner conflicts cause much of the fatigue we
feel and the weariness we fight because they burn up
so much of our energy. We noted that Jesus was a
person of limited energy just as we are. Yet He distin-

guished Himself in that He did not dissipate any of His energy on destructive emotions that foment inner hassles. Rather, He concentrated His energy singularly on the positive purposes God had called Him to pursue. And the point toward which we are driving in these two chapters is that Jesus can enable us to handle our hassles as He handled His. He will do that, if we will allow His Spirit to apply His power and pattern to our lives in the nitty-gritty of our daily experience. In the previous chapter we examined the first of three principles that enabled Jesus to handle His hassles: *He renounced His rights.* Now we continue with principles two and three: *Jesus renounced rigidity; Jesus renounced retreat.*

Renouncing Our Rigidity

To be rigid means to be stiff, uptight, inflexible, unyielding, severe, unteachable, unpliable. A rigid person is one who is obsessed with the need to be right even at the expense of being responsive to human hurts. A rigid person cannot adapt his convictions to the conditions called for in a given situation. He would rather express his convictions than his compassion.

In his book, *Run and Not Be Weary,* Dr. Dwight Carlson discusses the devastating toll rigidity takes upon a person. He identifies rigidness as one of the prime causes of emotional fatigue and demonstrates how an inflexible, unyielding, unpliable spirit impoverishes rigid people with spiritual weariness and despair.[1]

In the third chapter of his Gospel, Mark relates an incident that portrays Jesus in the presence of rigid

76

people. The situation called for compassion, flexibility and action on behalf of a desperate man whose hurts needed healing. But the fourth commandment of the Jewish law called for reverence on the Sabbath. All work was forbidden. And since healing the man's hurts could be construed as work, the man would have to leave the synagogue, hurts and all. But Jesus steps forth in the midst of these rigid people and renounces all identification with their rigidity. He pits the first commandment against the fourth and shows them that their compulsion to be right has actually led them into wrong.

Jesus exemplified compassion. He was a person with lofty convictions. He was God in the flesh, the human personification of God's truth and righteousness. Therefore, Jesus, more than anyone who ever walked this earth, was concerned for the right. Yet Jesus never allowed His convictions to short-circuit His compassion. He taught us that our highest duty is not to be right; our first responsibility is to love—to love God and to demonstrate our love for God by our love for one another. Therefore, when a brother or sister needed compassion, Jesus subjected His convictions to the compassion called for in the situation. He renounced rigidity. The rigid "uptightness" of His religious contemporaries was not for Him. He came with new wine and a new life-style of freedom and flexibility, compassion and pliability.

That is what made Jesus so winsome and popular with the common people of the land. People are drawn to a person who emanates vibrations of freedom, approachability, flexibility and love. They are attracted to that person like iron-filings to a magnet because that kind of free, open, adaptable, approachable, compassionate life-style emits signals of strength, acceptance and confidence.

The people knew the Pharisees were an uptight lot. Furthermore, they felt the side effects of the Pharisees' emotional/spiritual weariness. These side effects were fatigue and frustration, the direct descendants of their rigidity. For, the more weary the Pharisees became in their rigidity, the more they oppressed their contemporaries with their religious demands. But the people saw in Jesus a new wine, a wine they wanted to taste. For, though He was a person of impeccable convictions, He never allowed His convictions to smother His compassion. Though He was God's champion for right and truth, He never allowed His passion for the right to keep Him from responding to people's hurts.

As we sat at the end of the runway, with one plane after another taking off before us, I sensed something was wrong. Soon the captain's voice over the PA system confirmed my suspicions. One of the engines was functioning in reverse. So we had to return to the loading gate for repairs. Immediately a gray-haired businessman in the seat ahead of me began voicing his displeasure for everyone to hear. Soon the flight attendants came running to mollify his anger and reduce his temperature.

But he would have none of their apologies. He was important. And if he did not reach O'Hare Airport by such and such a time he would miss his flight to a crucial meeting in Philadelphia. Feeling the frustration of being snared in the vise of that unwelcome interruption, he got up and began pacing up and down the aisle, muttering to himself, clenching his fists, setting his jaw, showing his teeth, trying to recruit other passengers in his campaign of discontent. And before long, he began to display definite signs of fatigue. His face flushed, his chest began to heave deep sighs every few moments. Several physical signs indicated that his emotional/spiritual uptightness was taking a devastating toll on his whole being. And in the process he was communicating weariness to everyone around him.

In contrast to that childish display of rigidity, there sat beside me a young businessman from Holland— alert, sharp, warm and approachable. He had just finalized a large purchase of grain and soybeans in Minneapolis, a shipment which his company would market in Europe. He, too, had to make connections in Chicago. Only his flight was to Amsterdam, a much more delicate connection to make than to Philadelphia. Yet, in spite of circumstances similar to the man ahead of us, this man proved to be flexible and understanding. He was free to let other people fail. He did not view this mechanical failure as a threat. And as we conversed together during that hour's delay, I found myself drawing strength and energy from his disposition. His openness to the problem and his refreshing ability to roll with it communicated calmness and resilience to me.

Which of these two dispositions has the upper hand in your life? Your rigidity or your empathetic response to someone else's failure or hurt? Your need to express your convictions or your willingness to convey your compassion? Where do you find yourself? With the Pharisees or with Jesus? With the man ahead of me or the gentleman beside me? As you survey your actions in the heat of your current battles, do you observe a general tenor of rigidity and uptightness? Are you driven by your compulsion to be right no matter what, by your inner need to be meticulous, fastidious, perfectionistic? Or can you flex with your serendipities? Can you flow with your surprises?

A friend sent Bruce Larson the following wish one day, "May you always be young and glad, and even if it's Sunday, may you be wrong. For when men are always right, they are no longer young."[2]

Jesus offers us rest and freedom. Some of us are bone-weary. And we are communicating fatigue and frustration to people around us because of our rigidity, our uptightness, our need to be right and on-schedule no matter what, our compulsion to maintain our convictions at the expense of people who need our compassion. Jesus shows us a better way and invites us to walk in that way with Him. It was to these very uptight, rigid, inflexible Pharisees that Jesus said: "Come to me, all who labor and are heavy laden, and I will give you rest. Take my yoke upon you, and learn from me; for I am gentle and lowly in heart, and you will find rest for your souls. For my yoke is easy, and my burden is light" (Matt. 11:28-30).

Will you trade in the fatigue of your rigidity and the weariness of your uptightness for Christ's offer of rest and His life-style of freedom? He's available now to give you that chance if you'll take it.

There is a third principle Jesus personified in His life-style, a third principle that enabled Him to handle His hassles in a healthy way. He focused His limited supply of energy solely on the positive purposes God called Him to pursue. He did not dissipate it on the destructive emotions that take such a devastating toll on us. Why? First, because He renounced His rights; second, because He renounced rigidity; third because he renounced retreat.

Renouncing Retreat

Another of the major causes of our emotional/spiritual fatigue is our tendency to run away from our conflicts and from the people who precipitate them. And that retreat from hassles magnifies the fatigue it engenders in our lives.

But Jesus shows us a better way. He was not a peace-at-any-price person. Nor was He a people-pleaser. On the contrary, Jesus personified a life-style that dealt honestly and sensitively with the people who were creating conflicts and generating hassles for Him.

Jesus renounced retreat from His hassles. He cared enough to confront. He developed a technique for facing conflicts that David Augsburger calls "care-fronting,"[3] that is, confronting people in a way that brings both integrity and sensitivity to the surface of the relationship.

Notice how Jesus renounced retreat in the narrative before us. Weary from the demands of a heavy itinerary, Jesus slips into a synagogue on a Sabbath morning to worship with the others who had gathered there. But in that synagogue jammed with uptight, rigid, religious people was a common man with a heavy hurt on his heart. He had a deformed hand.

81

And the rigid, uptight watchdogs who barked at everything that wasn't kosher, watched Jesus intently. They glowered at Him with hate and venom in their eyes, waiting to see whether He would dare break the Sabbath by reaching out to heal this desperate man's hurts. If He did, they would have proof that He wasn't their Messiah. For their Messiah would obviously never do anything they thought was wrong. So they watched Him.

However, Jesus cared enough to confront. In full knowledge of the Pharisees' hostile inspection, Jesus proceeded to heal the man, Sabbath or no Sabbath. They had created a situation that was charged with the electricity of conflict. They had staged a heavy hassle for Jesus, and Jesus shows us how He handles His hassles.

Jesus does not back down from His hassles. He refuses to walk away. He renounces retreat. Rather, He cares enough to confront. And He confronts this conflict with both integrity and sensitivity. He is honest with Himself, with the crippled man and with His adversaries.

Yet Jesus declares His honest feelings and intentions in a very sensitive manner. He does not create a scene like the man in front of me on the plane. Jesus did not confront His conflicts because He wanted to tell people where to get off. He did not seek a platform for venting His spleen. On the contrary, He confronted His conflicts because He cared. He cared for that crippled man. He also cared for those uptight, rigid Pharisees whose hearts were crippled with hatred and insecurity. He cared enough for them to confront them honestly and sensitively.

This principle of renouncing retreat and caring enough to confront can be seen in almost every conflict Jesus faced. He cared enough to confront the boastful Simon when Simon claimed he would never forsake His Lord. He cared enough to confront the broken Simon after he had denied His Lord and cursed Him with blasphemous oaths.

These were painful confrontations for Jesus as well as for Simon. We would have let them pass, hoping the conflict with all of its hurts would simply go away. But Jesus cared too much for Simon and for the relationship He wanted to have with Simon to ignore the conflict. So He confronted him honestly and sensitively.

He cared enough to confront Judas around the table on that fateful night when Judas betrayed Him. Here again, Jesus confronted Judas because He cared. I believe He was giving Judas one last chance to recant, to scuttle his plot and pledge his allegiance to Jesus.

Jesus care-fronted Judas because He loved him. He cared enough to confront His mother when she was taking undue advantage of Him at the marriage at Cana (see John 2:34), and at Capernaum when she tried to interrupt His ministry (see Mark 3:31-35). He cared enough to confront His cross, the worst conflict of all. Luke tells us: "When the days drew near for him to be received up, he set his face to go to Jerusalem" (9:51).

Jesus renounced retreat. Regardless of the nature of the conflict invading Him, He did not withdraw. He refused to walk away and repress His feelings. On the contrary, He cared enough for the people and the relationships involved in every conflict to confront that conflict honestly and sensitively, with love and truth, with an open expression of His feelings and a compassionate commitment of Himself to the person or persons who were precipitating the conflict.

How different from the way most of us handle our hassles. Most of us deal with our conflicts by running away from them. We retreat behind the private walls of our defenses and pretend the conflict doesn't exist. We withdraw, give in and walk away angry, frustrated and wallowing in self-pity. We smile at our adversary while inside we are seething with resentment. Why?

Because we don't care enough for the people and the relationships involved to do something honest and sensitive about our conflicts. And because we don't care enough to confront, we burden ourselves with an unbearable load of weariness. It is the emotional/spiritual fatigue that weighs heavily upon all who run away from their hassles.

Jesus handled His hassles. He renounced retreat. He refused to run. Rather, He cared enough to confront. And because He did, three beautiful results had a chance to occur. First, the broken relationship had a chance to be mended. Second, His adversaries had a chance to become His friends. And third, His own being had a chance to throw off all destructive emotions that would rob Him of the energy He needed to pursue God's positive purposes for His life.

Jesus can help us handle our hassles. Howard Butt tells of the conflict that festered long and livid between his brother, Charles, and him. Their father had built a gigantic grocery chain in Texas and was stepping down, yielding control of the corporation to his sons. Howard was 10 years older than Charles. That gave Howard good reason to assume he was first in line for the top banana. But Howard's interest was divided between business and lay-preaching. He is an exceptional communicator, a Christian layman in great demand at retreats and conferences all across our country.

Charles, on the other hand, is just as committed to Christ, but thoroughly dedicated to business. He was the natural heir to dad's mantle at the helm of the company—sharp, tough, aggressive, yet kind—a real velvet-covered brick. But Howard was too jealous of Charles to let him lead. So the two brothers nursed that inner conflict until it marooned both of them in a stalemate of weariness, anger, resentment and unproductivity.

Then one morning, while he was reading the Bible, Howard Butt let Jesus get behind his private wall of defensiveness and probe the dirty depths of that family conflict. The Spirit of God convicted him of running away from the conflict, of refusing to care enough for his father and his brother to confront them honestly, sensitively, and confess his feelings to them.

Howard Butt tells how he got up off his knees, went to the office, confronted his father and brother, confessed his jealousy, admitted his feelings of hostility and rivalry and told them how much he cared for them and for the relationship he wanted to have with them. From that day to this, Howard Butt has been working for little brother Charles. And both of them have been running without weariness because they keep practicing Christ's principle of caring enough to confront whenever conflicts begin to surface between them.[4]

Do you want to handle your hassles as Jesus handled His? He dealt with His conflicts by renouncing His rights, by renouncing rigidity and by renouncing retreat. He is available right now to enable you to live by the very same power, practicing the same principles. Do you want His power and principles for your hassles? Or are you content to hang tough with your own proven methods? Will you let Him enable you to handle your hassles His way? If you will, tell Him so, right now.

Notes

1. Dwight Carlson, *Run and Not Be Weary* (Old Tappan, N.J.: Fleming H. Revell Co., 1974), pp. 113-115.
2. Bruce Larson, *Ask Me to Dance* (Waco: Word Books, 1972), p. 53.
3. David Augsburger, *Caring Enough to Confront* (Glendale, Calif.: Regal Books, 1973).
4. Howard Butt, *The Velvet Covered Brick* (New York: Harper and Row Publishers, 1973), pp. 5-7.

PROFITING FROM PRESSURE

8

And he told his disciples to have a boat ready
for him because of the crowd, lest they
should crush him; for he had healed many, so
that all who had diseases pressed upon him
to touch him (Mark 3:9,10).

A medical doctor made a shocking statement at a
dinner party he was attending. He was listening to a
public health nurse tell of her work among the Eskimos in northern Canada. She mentioned that, before the arrival of the white man, the Eskimos had not
had any serious mental or emotional disorders. But
now they were experiencing anxiety neuroses and
other emotional problems. When the doctor heard
this, he exclaimed, "That's wonderful! It's about time
they joined the human race!"[1]
The others in the group were stunned by his com-
ments. How could he be so cold and heartless? How
could he be so callous as to rejoice at the emotional
suffering of fellow human beings? But then they be-

gan to sense what he meant. He was calling attention to the fact that there is much more to living than simply the avoidance of problems. He was underscoring the truth that sometimes it is only in the heat of the problem, in the crucible of pressure, in the stress of trying circumstances, that we discover what it really means to be alive.

There are numerous clichés being bandied about these days concerning our culture. And, no matter which of these slogans future historians may choose to pin on us, one characteristic cannot be overlooked if we are to be portrayed accurately. That is, we are a people under pressure. Let's face it, we live in a pressure cooker. The anxiety-producing forces that invade our lives every day are intense and sometimes terribly threatening.

We are pressured on the job, pressured in the home, pressured at school, pressured at church. We are pressured by our parents, by our children, by our friends, by our competitors, by our enemies. We are pressured by schedules we can't meet, by circumstances we can't help, by pain and suffering we can't escape. We are pressured by what we hear, by what we see, by what we feel, by what we read. And, sometimes it seems that no matter where we go, what we do, or who we're with, we cannot throw off the nagging presence of pressure.

Pressure is not neutral. It never leaves us as it finds us. It always makes a deep impact on our lives. Either it propels us ahead or it pushes us back. Either it produces a positive increase or a negative decrease in our character. Either we profit from it, or we perish from it. And there are a great many people in our world who are literally perishing from pressure. Their hearts are failing them from fear. Not too long ago, U.S. Congressman William Mills blew his brains out under the duress of charges that he had accepted a $25,000 campaign contribution illegally. People are perishing from pressure.

There is a great deal we could say about the negative effects of the pressure under which we live day by day. But, I want to zero in on the positive, healthy value of all the stress we feel. Let us consider the ways you and I can profit from pressure. There are at least three reasons why pressure can be profitable to us.

Pressure Develops Our Resources

For many years, scientists have known that diamonds are fashioned in carbon deposits by extreme pressure from the earth's inner forces. This was demonstrated a few years ago when General Electric announced the successful development and production of "synthetic diamonds," which required a pressure of more than one-and-a-half million pounds per square inch at temperatures of 5,000 degrees Fahrenheit for hours at a time. It takes intense pressure and heat to fashion a diamond.

The principle of pressure is found in many areas of nature. We are told that nature produces coal and oil by exerting immeasurable stress upon accumulations of dead leaves and vegetation far below the ground. Moreover, a butterfly would never have the strength to fly if it were not allowed to gain that strength in its long and arduous work as a caterpillar pushing its way through the walls of its cocoon.

Remove the pressure from the caterpillar and you will have a butterfly that can't fly. Remove the pressure from those carbon deposits and you will have no coal, no oil, no diamonds. Nature supplies us with ample illustrations of the truth that pressure is profitable because it develops resources. Things that are valuable are produced under pressure.

And what is true of nature is also true of human nature. We, likewise, develop our resources under pressure. The story is told of a college student who was going to school and working part time to maintain his slender thread of survival. He had a job as an extra in an opera company. After spending the day in classes, he would play a bit part in the opera performance at night. Someone was discussing his rigorous schedule with him, and he said, "Oh, it's easy. All I have to do is carry a spear." An elderly woman became deeply concerned about him and asked, "How do you possibly stay awake after a whole day in school and such late hours at the opera?" He replied, "Oh, that's easy. The fellow behind me also carries a spear!"[2]

Pressure is profitable because it is often the only thing that keeps us going. It keeps jabbing us with its spear, thereby developing our resources of endurance. It keeps poking us with its relentless demands, thereby bringing out of us the sheer determination to stick with something until it's done.

Consider the severe strain to which Jesus was subjected immediately following His baptism. Mark tells us that Jesus was driven out into the wilderness by the Holy Spirit, into face-to-face confrontation with the devil. Why? In order that at the outset of His public ministry, Jesus might develop His resources for combating Satan.

The writer to the Hebrews tells us that Jesus "learned obedience through the things he suffered" (5:8). It was in the stress of those trying circumstances in the desert that Jesus Christ began to develop the resources—the physical, mental, emotional and spiritual resources—He would later need to smash His enemy. He learned obedience through suffering. He developed His resources under pressure and pain.

If Jesus found pressure profitable and necessary for the development of His resources, then the same must certainly be true of us. You and I are just like those raw carbon deposits buried far underground. And we will stay that way, just like a pile of dead leaves and vegetation, unless we are privileged to experience the intense pressure and heat of trying circumstances and painful discipline. We are like the caterpillar in the cocoon. And we will stay that way, just like a spineless worm, unless we are privileged to flex the muscles of our character against the walls of difficulty and hardship in this life.

Pressure is profitable for the development of our resources. Without the pressure of temptation, we would never develop the will to choose God's will. Without the pressure of life's rigorous schedule, we would never develop the discipline to spend our time wisely and profitably. Without the pressure of pain and suffering, we would never develop a keen sense of need for God and for one another.

The story is told of some peasant farmers in Germany who were distressed by several years of poor harvests. So they made a bargain with the Lord. They asked Him to give them exactly what they requested for one year. And He agreed to their bargain. When the farmers prayed for rain, He sent rain. When they asked for sun, He sent sun. Never did their crops grow so tall and their fruit trees so leafy.

But when harvest time came, their delight turned to dismay. For, they discovered that there was no corn or grain on the stalks and no fruit in the orchard. What went wrong? Had God failed them? Not at all. He granted their every request during that growing season. The trouble was that they did not ask for the harsh north winds. And of course without the winds there was no pollination.[3]

When golf balls were first manufactured, they were made with smooth covers. Then it was discovered that after a ball had been roughed up, it would travel a greater distance. Hence they started manufacturing them with dimpled covers.[4] So it is with life. It takes some rough spots in life to make you go your farthest. Pressure is profitable because it develops the resources that enable you to go the distance.

Pressure Determines Our Reality

There is a very significant verse in Luke's Gospel. Jesus said, "The good news of the kingdom of God is preached, and every one enters it violently" (16: 16). Jesus is saying, "Every one who enters the Kingdom of God does so with violence." The phrase *with violence* can also be translated "under pressure." What does Jesus mean by that? Simply this. There is nothing like pressure to separate the man from the boy, the real from the unreal, the genuine from the phony, the true from the false, the authentic from the counterfeit.

Some time ago, I was conversing with a friend who happens to be a fireman. I asked him how they separate the applicants in their candidate school in order to eliminate the potentially incompetent firemen. He replied that the final test was to put all the trainees in a garage, close the doors, and then ignite the garage with a slow, smoking fire. And the last ones to flee that smoke-filled garage were accepted as potentially good firemen. Why? Because they proved in the crucible of pressure, in the stress of trying circumstances, in the nausea of that smoldering environment, that their intentions were real. Their endurance of that pressure determined the reality of their claim. They wanted to be firemen and they were willing to pay the price.

Jesus claims that we enter the Kingdom of God in the same way. By faith, to be sure, but by faith that is real. "The good news of the Kingdom of God is preached, and every one who enters it must do so 'under pressure.' "

Pressure is profitable because it determines our reality as Christians. Our response to the pressures of life shows us more than anything else, whether we are trusting in God or trusting in ourselves. Pressure has a way of determining our reality. Its heat separates the real from the unreal, the genuine from the phony, the authentic from the counterfeit.

In Mark 4:16,17, Jesus says, "And these in like manner are the ones sown upon rocky ground, who, when they hear the word, immediately receive it with joy; and they have no root in themselves, but endure for a while; then, when tribulation or persecution arises on account of the word, immediately they fall away."

The apostle Peter spoke of the value of pressure in his first letter to Christians of his day. Peter wrote, "Now for a little while you may have to suffer various trials, so that your faith may be proved genuine" (see 1 Pet. 1:6).

Then Peter adds this perspective: "Rejoice when you're under pressure. Thank God for the stress, because that stress is going to determine the reality of your claim to faith in Christ" (see 1 Pet. 1:6,7).

One evening Ole Bull, the famous Norwegian violinist, was giving a concert at the Opera House in Paris when the A string on his instrument broke. Without hesitating he transposed the difficult composition into another key and finished the concert on three strings. A lesser violinist might have stopped and grumbled about his bad luck. But it takes a great artist to say, "If I can't play on four strings, I will play on three."[5] The unbelievable pressure of that crisis proved the greatness of that violinist. It demonstrated the reality of his talent.

So it is with us when pressure invades our lives. It determines our reality. It divulges the truth about us. It uncovers the source of our confidence. It exposes the roots of our trust.

Pressure Demands Our Retreat

There is an old proverb that says, "If you can't stand the heat, then get out of the kitchen." How true! That truth is borne out in what we have just said about pressure determining our reality.

But, there is another side to this coin, too. There are times when none of us can stand the heat any longer. We need a breather, a respite, a time to relax and recover and recuperate from the stress of life. Our success-oriented society lives by the maxim that, under pressure, strong men produce and weak men collapse. And, for the most part, that maxim proves true. But it is also true that the pressures of life will break even the strongest of us unless we yield to their demands for relief.

History tells us the sad story of many strong men (even strong men of God) who capsized under pressure. Men like Samson, Saul, David, Peter, Demas and even the incomparable Moses caved in on at least one momentous occasion.

During the many interviews reporters had with the POW's who returned from Hanoi, one question was often asked: "Why did you yield to the enemy's pressure and sign those phony statements of confession?"

After the men described the torturous pressures to which they had been subjected before they signed those statements, they said, "You can endure it only so long. Every man has his breaking point some place, some time."

How true that is! Even the strongest of us must retreat from the squeeze on a regular basis, or we will break under the strain. Therefore, this represents another reason why pressure is profitable—because it demands release. It forces us to run for cover.

Jesus knew what it meant to run for cover. In the previous chapter we noted that Jesus never retreated from His hassles. He cared enough to confront people with sensitivity and integrity. He refused to retreat from conflict. But, He did retreat from pressure when He sensed He was nearing the breaking point. Mark says, "And he told his disciples to have a boat ready for him because of the crowd, lest they should crush him; for he had healed many, so that all who had diseases pressed upon him to touch him" (Mark 3:9, 10).

The people were pressing upon Jesus with such frantic intensity that He knew He must get out of there before He collapsed under the stress. So He ordered His disciples (Matthew 14:22 says, "He made the disciples") to prepare a boat for His departure. And, Jesus, the Son of God, ran for cover. He escaped from pressure.

There is nothing wrong with escaping from pressure. The point is how you escape. If you escape into alcohol, drugs, self-pity, material indulgence, pleasure or suicide, that is unfortunate because you never find relief, just more pressure. But if you escape as Jesus did, then you will find relief. He sought physical relief by changing His environment. He split the scene. He sought emotional release by exchanging the noise of the crowd for the quietness of solitude. And He sought spiritual retreat by opening His life to His Father in prayer.

Sometimes Jesus found prayer to be very excruciating, such as in Gethsemane. But most often, He discovered it to be His most refreshing means of release from the stresses that pressed Him. The pressure of His life was profitable because it forced Him to run to His Father for cover.

Sometimes Jesus couldn't stand the heat in the kitchen any longer. He had to get out. There are times when none of us can stand the heat either. We, too, need to run, sometimes for our very lives. Therefore, pressure can be exceedingly profitable in our lives if it forces us to seek our relief where Jesus sought His, in communion with His Father. He retreated physically, emotionally and spiritually. And when He did He always returned refreshed and ready for action, prepared for pressure.

May God enable you to find profit in the pressure you face as that pressure develops your resources, determines your reality and demands your retreat. Pressure will definitely do something to you. The question is: What will you do with it?

Notes

1. Bruce Larson, *Setting Men Free* (Grand Rapids: Zondervan Publishing House, 1967), p. 19.
2. Richard Woodsome, "Man's Oldest Question," *Pulpit Digest* (May 1971), p. 47.
3. Told by Robert Schuller in *You Can Become the Person You Want to Be* (New York: Hawthorn Books, 1973), p. 161.
4. Charles Allen, *All Things Are Possible Through Prayer* (Old Tappan, N.J.: Fleming H. Revell Co., 1958), p. 84.
5. Gaston Foote, *How God Helps* (Nashville: Abingdon Press, 1966), p. 61.

9
DARING
TO
SHARE

And they went to a place which was called Gethsemane; and he said to his disciples, "Sit here, while I pray." And he took with him Peter and James and John, and began to be greatly distressed and troubled. And he said to them, "My soul is very sorrowful, even to death; remain here, and watch." And going a little farther, he fell on the ground and prayed that, if it were possible, the hour might pass from him. And he said, "Abba, Father, all things are possible to thee; remove this cup from me; yet not what I will, but what thou wilt." And he came and found them sleeping, and he said to Peter, "Simon, are you asleep? Could you not watch one hour? Watch and pray that you may not enter into temptation; the spirit indeed is willing, but the flesh is weak." And again he went away and prayed, saying the same words. And again he came and found them sleeping, for their eyes were very heavy; and they did not know what to answer him. And he came the third time, and said to them, "Are you still sleeping and taking your rest? It is enough; the hour has come; the Son of man is betrayed into the hands of sinners. Rise, let us be going; see, my betrayer is at hand" (Mark 14:32-42).

Dwight Carlson is a doctor of internal medicine and an outstanding Christian layman. He is the brother of the famous Dr. Paul Carlson, who was martyred in the Congo in 1964. Dwight Carlson's practice of internal medicine brings him into daily contact with people who are suffering the effects of emotional exhaustion and spiritual fatigue. He has written a book about his experience, a book in which he shares the Christian answer to fatigue.

According to Dr. Carlson, one of the heavy causes of psychological/spiritual weariness is our unwillingness to remove our masks and live with each other as real people. He writes:

Like all other unresolved internal conflicts, the mask requires a lot of energy and leads to a host of problems besides fear, such as irritability, worry, anxiety, fatigue, excusing ourselves, blaming others, and, not infrequently, frank lying and deceit.[1]

Remove Your Mask

Dr. Carlson's personal experience with hundreds of patients has convinced him that the masks we maintain, the personages we project, the walls we erect and the defenses we deploy are roadblocks on the path to freedom from fatigue. We can never really throw off the burden we carry, the fatigue we feel and the weariness we fight until we dare to walk out (or at least peek out occasionally) from behind the masks we wear.

Jesus personified the life-style that was free of fatigue. Why? Because He was free of all masks. He lived His life in the open, especially with three men who became His "kinship circle." Simon Peter, James, John and Jesus became the first Christian cell group. With those three men Jesus shared everything about Himself. He held nothing back. In the vernacular of our day, "He let it all hang out." It was to those three men, and only to them, that Jesus revealed His power on that day when He raised Jairus' daughter from the dead. Mark 5:37 says, "And he allowed no one to follow him [into the house where the girl was lying] except Peter and James and John the brother of James."

Likewise, it was to those three men, and only to them, that Jesus revealed His glory on the Mount of Transfiguration. Again Mark says, "And after six days Jesus took with him Peter and James and John, and led them up a high mountain apart by themselves; and he was transfigured [glorified] before them" (9:2).

The Gospel writers are careful to record that these momentous occasions in the life of Jesus were shared with the three members of His "kinship circle." He opened His innermost being to Peter, James and John, showing them awesome revelations of His power and glory.

Now, in this regard, Jesus has nothing on any of us. We, too, are most ready and willing to dazzle people with whatever power and glory we might be able to put on display. Ours may not be the power of resurrection or the glory of transfiguration. But we are quite prepared, even anxious, to open ourselves and display our modest powers and glories to anyone who will look and listen. Therefore, in this respect, Jesus lived no more openly than any of us. But this is where we part company with Him.

Share Your Unacceptable Hurt

The paragraph from Mark's Gospel at the outset of this chapter gives us a glimpse of yet another time when Jesus opened Himself and shared His inner being with His three confidants. This occasion does not display Jesus in dazzling form. There is no power and no glory here. But that's the point, the very point the Gospel writers take pains to communicate.

It was the eve of His crucifixion. Jesus and His eleven faithful followers had just spent several hours together in a room where they shared a very special meal. Now the hour is late. He has led the eleven to a place called Gethsemane, a garden where He often retreated for prayer. As they entered the garden, Jesus asked eight of His disciples to wait near the gate. Then, as was His custom, He took with Him the inner three—Simon Peter, James and John. And the four members of that intimate inner circle went far into the garden by themselves.

Have you ever wondered why Jesus took Peter, James and John with Him? Why did He not leave all eleven at the gate? The answer is obvious in the text. Jesus thirsted for their fellowship in this dark hour of His life. These three men had shared intimately with

Jesus in times of His power and glory. Now Jesus wanted them to be with Him in a time of hurt and heartbreak. For, Mark claims, as soon as Jesus got alone with Peter, James and John, "He began to be greatly distressed and troubled." The *New English Bible* puts it like this: "horror and dismay came over him."

The moment the four of them retreated to a spot where they could be alone, Jesus stepped out from behind His mask of serenity and calm, and fell apart. And as He opened His innermost person to His three trusted companions, His feelings came gushing out of Him in a torrent of emotion. He started sharing with them the "unacceptable hurts" of His inner life. And He said, "My heart is ready to break with grief. Remain here and watch. I am coming unglued with anxiety about my cross. Stay close enough to me so I can sense the strength of your empathy."

Entering the garden a little farther, Jesus fell on the ground and prayed. The Gospel writers tell us that Jesus interrupted His prayer three different times, returning to His three friends to share more of His hurts with them and to draw strength from their empathy. The fact that those three privileged companions failed Jesus in this crisis does not alter the intent or the impact of Christ's actions in Gethsemane. Jesus shows Himself to be the Servant who was willing to open Himself to His friends that they might see and know and share in the raw reality of His unmentionable tensions, His undiscussable anxieties, His unacceptable hurts.

We recoil from this dimension of Christ's life-style. We are prepared to share our displays of power and glory with anyone who will look and listen. Some of us are even willing to share our "acceptable hurts" with a few intimate friends. But the vast majority of us are not at all willing to share our "unacceptable hurts" with anyone, not even our spouses. We would rather be fatigued than be free of our mask. Christ's conduct in Gethsemane is unacceptable conduct in our society. It is unacceptable conduct among friends, in many families. Yes, and it is unacceptable conduct even in most churches.

From our earliest years of childhood we are taught that our unacceptable hurts must be shielded from other people at all costs. Recently I heard of a little girl who fell in a supermarket and skinned her knee badly. She broke into a piercing wail and her mother rushed over and said, "Oh Mary, don't cry here where people can see you!"

If ever there was a slogan that fits our society, both outside and inside the church, that's it. "Don't cry here where people can see you." Americans are forbidden to share their unacceptable hurts and their unmentionable sins even with close friends. We must not be caught crying where people can see us.

In this respect we are much more like Adolph Hitler than Jesus Christ. Albert Speer's *Inside the Third Reich* was greeted by *The New York Times* as "a unique portrait of Hitler, one that is unlikely ever to be surpassed." In Nazi Germany, Albert Speer was Hitler's chief architect, Minister of Armaments and a member of Hitler's inner circle of power. Yet this is what Speer says about his Fuehrer:

> Sometimes I asked myself: Why can't I call
> Hitler my friend? What is missing? I spent

103

endless time with him, was almost at home in his private circle and, moreover, his foremost associate in his favorite field, architecture. Everything was missing. Never in my life have I met a person who so seldom revealed his feelings, and if he did so, instantly locked them away again. During my time in Spandau I talked with Hess about this peculiarity of Hitler's. Both of us agreed that there had been moments when we felt we had come close to him. But we were invariably disillusioned. If either of us ventured a slightly more personal tone, Hitler promptly put up an unbreakable wall.[2]

What a portrait of the emotional ideal the average American male is striving for today. To be unexpressive! To keep the lid clamped tightly on all unacceptable feelings and hurts. To be chic, suave, debonair, cool, sophisticated, blasé, urbane and polished. To have it all together, to be able to dazzle our peers with our power and glory.

But what about those times when we don't have it all together? Sometimes, as with Jesus in Gethsemane, we feel like we're coming apart. What about those times in our lives? Do we still try to act cool? If we do, we become the victims of psychological/spiritual exhaustion. Why? Because we waste all our energy trying to hold the lid on, trying to act cool when we're burning up.

Why was Jesus able to walk out of Gethsemane into the teeth of the foulest treatment anyone has ever experienced? What gave Him the strength to face the cross with its sin and shame and almighty wrath? It was Christ's willingness to be weak before God and before those three intimate friends. It was His readiness to be open before them, to share His unacceptable hurts with them. And out of that experience of openness with God and man—out of that sharing of unacceptable hurts—out of that crucible of weakness came the strength Christ needed for the cross.

As it was with Jesus so it must be with us. Healing comes to our troubled souls only when we are willing to share our unacceptable hurts with God and with a group of people who play a significant role in our lives. Strength to face the crises we think are unfaceable comes when we are ready to be weak with God and with a circle of friends who will let us be what we really are.

Relinquish Your Pride

What keeps us from that strength? What keeps us from sharing our unacceptable hurts with a cell group of people who long to bear our cares? What keeps us bound in our fatigue behind our mask of sophistication? Is it not our pride? The following allegory brings the issue into clear focus.

> The scene didn't make sense. There he lay in the street, bleeding—the hit-and-run driver gone. He needed medical help immediately! Yet he kept pleading. "Don't take me to the hospital, please!" Surprised, everyone asked why. Pleadingly he answered, "Because I'm on the staff at the hospital. It would be embarrassing for them to see me like this. They've never seen me bleeding and dirty.

They always see me clean and healthy; now I'm a mess."

"But the hospital is for people like you! Can't we call an ambulance?"

"No, please don't. I took a Pedestrian Safety Course, and the instructor would criticize me for getting hit."

"But who cares what the instructor thinks? You need attention . . . "

"Just pull me over to the curb. I'll make it some way. It's my fault that I got hit." With this, he tried to crawl to the gutter while everyone left, leaving him alone. Maybe he made it, maybe he didn't. Maybe he's still trying to stop his own bleeding.

Does that strike you as a strange, ridiculous story? It could happen any Sunday in a typical church. I know it could happen, because last night I asked some active Christians what they would do if on Saturday night they got hit and run over by some unacceptable sin. Without exception they said, "I sure wouldn't want to go to church the next morning, where everybody would see me." Is the church really going to be the church until every Christian, hit and run over by some sin, starts pleading, "Take me to the church. My brothers and sisters are there.

They care for me. I can get well there. And I know they won't talk about me when it's over."[3]

What a challenge to our pride. To come to church when we have been run over by some unacceptable hurt and to find a core group of people who care enough to bear our hurt and to be God's medicine for our healing. What a challenge to our pride, our coolness, our apathy, our sophistication! And just such a hurt-healing, need-meeting ministry happens in some churches every week. Our congregation has many kinship groups for adults that meet regularly. Cell groups where people can bring their unacceptable hurts, their undiscussable problems, their unmentionable sins and find acceptance from peers who care for them, dirt and hurt and all.

Are you part of a group like that? If not, why not? Jesus was! Could it be because of your pride, your preference for your mask with all of its fatigue?

Reach Out to Your Peers

Some of us are very willing to bear other people's burdens, but not willing to share our own. Some of us pride ourselves on the way we respond to the needs of the unfortunate. Many of us support orphans overseas and all manner of charities here at home. And that is good. Not for a moment would I want anyone to think I am not in favor of that. I am intensely involved in those kinds of ministries.

But, the point I am making is that all of these forms of "outreach" are not actually outreach at all. They are "down-reach." All of our outreach to the unfortunate is, in fact "down-reach." We are reaching down

107

to people who have less than we have. And in that sense, though our motives may be beautiful, we are sharing with them a dazzling display of our power and our glory. And they are both impressed and appreciative.

But my question is: Can we who are so adept at reaching down also reach out from behind our masks and hand a group of our peers some of our unacceptable hurts, some of our undiscussable problems? That is "outreach" in the truest sense of the word. Outreach begins when I am willing to reach out from behind my defenses, hand you my soul with all of its dirt and hurt, and ask you to care for me, love me, accept me and help me in my weakness. Dare we share what we really are with a few people who would like to know us? Or must we spend our lives simply sharing what we have—our power and glory—with people who are less fortunate?

Bruce Thielemann tells of a painful experience he suffered with high school and college students of a church he served as pastor. Those young people taught him a tremendous truth. Thielemann says, "They showed me that I loved them enough to care for them. But I didn't love them enough to let them care for me."[4]

That is the gist of what I am trying to say to you. Do you love some people enough to let them care for you? Jesus did. He loved Simon Peter, James and John so much that He opened Himself to them in Gethsemane and gave them the opportunity to care for Him. Jesus did not come across as Mr. Cool. On the contrary, He shared with those three men His unacceptable hurts. He not only loved them enough to care for them. He loved them enough to let them care for Him. Do you love a group of people that much? There are people around you who would love to show you how much they care for you if you would let them. But you've got to be willing to be weak and vulnerable. Before they can bear your hurts, you've got to share your hurts with them honestly and openly.

Are you feeling fatigue and fighting weariness? If so, the chief cause could be all the energy you are wasting in your struggle to clamp the lid on your hurts. You will never really throw off your burden until you walk out from behind your mask in the presence of God and a group of friends. And as you let them see, know and share in the raw reality of your unacceptable hurts, your weariness will be transformed into energy. As you love them enough to let them care for the real you, your fatigue will flee in the wake of new freedom. May the Lord Jesus Christ motivate you to take advantage of this powerful possibility.

Notes

1. Dwight Carlson, *Run and Not Be Weary* (Old Tappan, N.J.: Fleming H. Revell Co., 1974), p. 65.
2. Albert Speer, *Inside the Third Reich* (New York: Macmillan Publishing Co., Inc., 1970), pp. 148, 149. Used by permission.
3. Told by Ray Stedman in the message, "When Rite Is Wrong" (Palo Alto: Discovery Publishing), p. 3.
4. Bruce Thielemann, "Grils," a message delivered at Bethel Theological Seminary, St. Paul, Minn.

10
FRIENDSHIP IS FOR SHARING

Brethren, if a man is overtaken in any trespass, you who are spiritual should restore him in a spirit of gentleness. Look to yourself, lest you too be tempted. Bear one another's burdens, and so fulfill the law of Christ. For if any one thinks he is something, when he is nothing, he deceives himself (Gal. 6:1-3).

Charles Francis Potter tells of the time his family moved into a rather snobbish neighborhood where his children weren't accepted. So they formed a backyard club of their own and invited some kids from the wrong side of the tracks to play with them. Soon they were having so much fun that the neighborhood children came and asked to join their club. Potter saw his son Myron look one of them over very carefully. Then he heard him say to that neighbor boy, "No, you must go on home. Nobody can belong to this club unless he has patches on his pants."

How similar to the church of Jesus Christ! The

church is not a club, to be sure. It is a body of believers whose head is Christ. It is an organism of people who share one thing in common: none of them has it all together; none of them can make it on his own. They all have patches in their lives. But their redeeming quality is that they know it, and they have given their torn, worn, broken, patched lives to Jesus, whose death and resurrection brings them healing for today and hope for tomorrow.

Lloyd Ogilvie, senior pastor of First Presbyterian Church of Hollywood, received a letter recently that said, "That church is filled with hypocrites!" Ogilvie wrote back, "That's true, and its saving grace is that some of them know it. Come join us; there's always room for one more!"[1]

The Patches

The church of Jesus Christ is a unique body of people. Unique, not because we all have patches in our lives; for, if the truth were known, all people everywhere have patches. But the church is unique in that every member knows his patches, admits them and experiences Christ's mending and healing by showing those patches to Him and to His people. It is this latter matter to which the apostle Paul addresses our attention in the opening verses of Galatians 6.

Our patches are our failures, our hurts, our burdens, our sins, all the things in our lives that have us hanging on the ropes in fatigue, weariness and defeat. Up to this point in our discussion of the Bible's antidote for fatigue we have majored on the primary issue: the urgent need for each of us to show our

111

patches to Christ and cast those burdens on Him.

There is a sense in which much of what has been said in this book could be summarized in the words of the psalmist, "Cast your burden on the Lord, and he will sustain you" (Ps. 55:22). That has been the major theme thus far, and it's still the theme. But in the previous chapter, the theme took a slightly different twist: the New Testament emphasis on casting our burdens on one another as well as on Christ.

Therefore, the Old Testament exhortation to cast our burdens upon the Lord is fulfilled in the New Testament exhortation to cast our burdens upon the Lord who is living in the brothers and sisters with whom we share our hurts and to whom we show our patches.

The point of the previous chapter is that freedom from fatigue comes only when we are willing to step out from behind our defenses and show our patches to some brothers and sisters who become Christ's instruments of healing for us. Now, in this chapter, I want to lead you farther down that road.

In Galatians 6:1-3, Paul placards before us the command Jesus issued regarding our need to share our hurts with each other and to bear those hurts for each other. Paul says (in paraphrase), "Brothers [and sisters], if any one is overtaken in any trespass, you who are spiritual should restore him in a spirit of gentleness. Look to yourself, lest you, too, be tempted. Bear one another's burdens, and so fulfill the law of Christ [the law of love that Christ laid on us when He said, 'Love one another as I have loved you']. For if any one thinks he is something, when he is nothing, [if anyone is foolish enough to think he has no patches on his pants] he deceives himself [and only himself]."

Those verses contain two Ps. First, there's the *Principle*. Then there's the *Process*.

The Principle

The principle is enunciated clearly in verse 2, "Bear one another's burdens, and so fulfill the law of Christ."

According to John 13:34, the "law of Christ" is the new law of love. Jesus commands us to love one another as He has loved us. We are to care for each other with the tender loving care we receive from Christ. Then, in Galatians 6:2, we fulfill the law of Christ (the law of love) by bearing one another's burdens. We put flesh and blood on Christ's command by caring enough for another Christian to take his burden from him and bear it for him. That is the principle enunciated here. It is a law, the only law, Jesus enforces on His followers. And as a law it becomes an obligation for us, never an option. We are obliged to care for our Christian brothers and sisters enough to take their burdens from them and bear those burdens for them.

There is a disease creeping dangerously through the church at large today. It is the disease of privatism. The disease of privatism rears its ugly head wherever people grow weary of the patches they dislike in the lives of their fellow Christians. These people decide to pull out of that body and form a pure group of their own for "we four and no more." But the tragedy of that exclusivism is its contradiction of everything Christian.

113

Francis Schaeffer was the first to grip me with the conviction that Christianity is personal but not private when he said:

> Salvation, as I have emphasized already, is individual, but not individualistic. People cannot become Christians except one at a time, and yet our salvation is not solitary. God's people are called together in community.[2]

That's it! To become a member of the body of Christ, each of us must have a personal experience with Jesus. We must individually invite Him into our lives and allow Him to become our Lord and Saviour. No one can do that for us.

But while our entrance into the body is personal, our life within the body can never be private. It can never become an exclusivistic, individualistic, private thing.

To be a Christian means to be a member of the Body of Christ, grafted in by the Holy Spirit at the moment of conversion. To be a member of Christ's body means to live in relationship with other Christians. We cannot remain in isolation. We are given responsibility for one another. We must accept that responsibility for one another or forfeit our claim to be a part of the body. To accept responsibility for one another means to bear each other's burdens, to care for another Christian enough to take his burdens from him and carry them for him.

But how do we follow the principle articulated here? How do we bear another Christian's burdens in a way that really brings freedom and release to him and not simply glory and ego satisfaction to ourselves? How do we do that? There is a sense in which the principle succeeds only in arousing either pride or guilt. Pride in those who think they are scoring well in the ministry of burden-bearing. And guilt in those who know they are not.

The Process

Paul outlines this real hurt-healing, need-meeting, soul-restoring, burden-bearing process. His instructions are eminently practical in this passage. He surrounds the principle with the process. He doesn't just exhort us to bear our brother's burdens. He explains how to do it in a way that really heals our brother's hurts, meets his needs and restores him to forgiveness and fellowship, to freedom from guilt, to the joy and zeal of a new beginning.

Here's how we do it. We share our hurts with the brother who is hurting. We show our patches to the brother who thinks he is the only one who has any. We identify with him at the point of his pain. This is what Paul meant by "restore him in a spirit of gentleness." Paul calls upon the "spiritual" members in a local body of believers to become the leaders, the vanguard troops in a ministry of restoration. "Brothers [and sisters], if any one is overtaken in any trespass, you who are spiritual should restore him in a spirit of gentleness. Look to yourself, lest you, too, be tempted" (see Gal. 6:1).

Who are the "spiritual" whom Paul calls to action? Are they the pompous, self-righteous, better-than-thou, wrist-slapping, finger-pointing, judgmental people every church seems to have? Hardly! They could never undertake a ministry of restoration.

115

First, because they are not spiritual, and then, because no one with a problem would ever come near them.

Well then, who are the "spiritual"? The clue to their identity is found in the closing sentence of verse 1 and in the explanation in verse 3. "Look to yourself, lest you too be tempted. Bear one another's burdens, and so fulfill the law of Christ. For if any one thinks he is something, when he is nothing, he deceives himself."

The "spiritual" are the members of the body who are painfully aware of all the patches they have on their pants. And they have brought them to Christ and to His people, have opened their lives before them, have shown their patches and shared their hurts, and have sought Christ's forgiveness and restoration through Christ's people in that place. That is why they can be gentle. That is the only reason they can deal with their broken, bleeding and burdened brothers in a spirit of gentleness.

They can be gentle because they are painfully aware of their own failures, their own sins and their own need of God's grace and forgiveness. It is "spiritual" people like that whom Paul calls into the forefront of a soul-restoring, hurt-healing, burden-bearing ministry within the Body of Christ. And the process he outlines for them to follow is one of sharing.

Paul Tournier, the eminent Swiss physician whose prolific writings plumb the depths of this issue, shares this personal note:

> The people who have helped me most are not
> those who have answered my confessions

with advice, exhortation or doctrine, but rather those who have listened to me in silence, and then told me of their own personal life, their own difficulties and experiences. [3]

I, too, have found this to be true in my experience. In our previous parish was a young family whose husband and father was an undercover agent for the sheriff's department. By the very nature of his work, that young man was exposed to life in many of its raunchiest forms. And after a while, the daily exposure to wickedness began to take its toll on him spiritually and emotionally. I knew him well enough to see this happening to him, but said nothing.

Then, after many months in a spiritual tailspin, he showed up in my office one day, unannounced. He sat down, his face lined with guilt, his cheeks ashen with shame and began to talk. At first his speech was very guarded, couched in vague generalities. Then gradually he grew more specific. He told me of the tremendous temptations to which he was being subjected and what they were doing to him and his marriage. And I listened, quite unshocked by his story.

When he finished I made no comment about what he had said. I simply began to share with him some of my temptations in those same areas and some of my failures. And as I showed him my patches, his eyes grew bigger by the minute. Then I told him how I showed those patches to Christ in the presence of my wife, Rae Ann. I told him how I had confessed those failures to her and had received Christ's forgiveness through her. And as I told him how Jesus was using Rae Ann to restore my soul, heal my hurts and bear my burdens, the color began to return to his cheeks. The contagious smile that used to grace his face reappeared after an absence of many months. He began to see how Christ could forgive his sins, take his guilt and restore his soul through the ministry of his own wife. If only he would ask her to bear this burden for him.

Several months ago, during a week Rae Ann and I spent in that community, that young man and his wife were among many old friends with whom we enjoyed an evening. At one point in the evening when others were engrossed in conversation, he met me at the punch bowl, put his massive hand on my shoulder and said, "Ross, I do not remember one thing you said in all those sermons you preached. Not one thing!"

That is not the kind of comment a pastor finds terribly encouraging. Then he added, "But what I do remember is that time in your office. I will never forget how you shared your failures with me. It made all the difference in the direction of my life."

By that statement he was simply bearing witness to the truth Paul underscores in Galatians 6:1-3. God gives each of us a ministry to our brothers and sisters in the body. It is the ministry of restoring their souls, healing their hurts and bearing their burdens. But how can we do that in a way that brings healing to them and not just ego-strength to us? How can we reach out to them without reaching down? Here's how! We do it "in a spirit of gentleness."

And how does that spirit of gentleness express itself? By our sensitivity to our own patches. By our willingness to share our hurts with a brother or sister who is hurting. By our willingness to show our patches to the one who thinks he is the only one who has any. By our ability to identify with him at the point of his pain and to show him how we entered into a personal experience of God's love through Christ, in spite of ourselves. That process of gentle openness is guaranteed to heal a brother's hurts and restore his troubled soul.

Testimonies to the effectiveness of this process of gentle, open sharing come from many voices in the Body of Christ today. Keith Miller tells of the first group he ever attended for the purpose of communicating with other Christians at a level below the surface. These were people who had been attending the same church for years, and yet who knew virtually nothing about each other's personal feelings and personal struggles. They spent that evening sharing their joys, triumphs and happy experiences of life.

As they were about to end that session and go their separate ways, a young woman about 30 years old said, "Wait a minute. I haven't said anything." And she was right. She had been so quiet they all had forgotten she was there. Looking painfully uneasy she finally spoke up and said, "I've been sitting here feeling awful. I don't have anything in common with you." And she proceeded to draw several contrasts between their joys and her frustrations, their triumphs and her trials, their victories and her failures, their happiness and her humdrum. Then in conclusion she paused, looked down and said simply, "I guess I want what you already have." And Keith Miller says:

We sat there, stunned by the reality which had drawn us irresistibly toward this thin, totally unprotected young woman, and I realized that it was *we* who needed what *she* had—the ability to be personal and honest in a vulnerable way. As I looked around at the group, I knew that somehow, because this theologically unsophisticated young woman had turned loose of her silence and her pride and reached out in total honesty, it was at last safe for us to start becoming one in Jesus Christ.

A change came over the group right then. Some people confessed that they hadn't been totally honest about things being so perfect in their lives. And as we let down the unreal walls of our perfections, several very striking things began to happen that night and in the weeks and months which followed.[4]

Strange, isn't it? What motivates our brothers and sisters to share their burdens with us is our willingness to share ours with them. What prompts them to show their inner patches to us is our willingness to show ours to them. Yet this really isn't so strange after all. For these are the very dynamics in the process of restoration described in Galatians 6:1-3.

The great untapped resource that can enable Christ's people to live beyond fatigue in this fatigue-inducing age is the soul-restoring, hurt-healing, burden-bearing ministry we can render to each other. The principle is clear. We must bear one another's burdens or we fail to fulfill Christ's law of love. The process is equally clear. We begin to bear a brother's burden not by accentuating his weakness or focusing on his failure. We begin to bear his burden by showing him our patches, by focusing on our failures, by identifying with his weaknesses, and by sharing with him what Christ has done for us in spite of ourselves. Will you hear the Word of the Lord? God wants to use your fertilizer to grow your brother's spirit. Will you let Him do that?

Notes

1. Lloyd John Ogilvie, *You've Got Charisma* (Nashville: Abingdon Press, 1975), p. 150.
2. Francis Schaeffer, *The Church at the End of the Twentieth Century* (Downers Grove, Ill.: Inter-Varsity Press, 1970), p. 60.
3. Paul Tournier, *The Meaning of Persons* (New York: Harper and Row Publishers, Inc., 1973), p. 191.
4. Keithe Miller, *The Becomers* (Waco: Word Books, 1973), p. 20. Used by permission.

11
THE HIGHWAY TO HEALING

> Therefore confess your sins to one another,
> and pray for one another, that you may be
> healed. The prayer of a righteous man has
> great power in its effects (Jas. 5:16).

Norman is one of God's unique and delightful servants. For many years he has been head of the world's largest faith missionary agency. He tells of the time he was in Uganda during the great Christian revival there. Observing the genuineness of those Ugandan Christians in their repentance before God and their confession to one another, he was convicted of his own sham and pretense. One night after spending several hours with those open, humble, vulnerable Ugandans, Norman returned to his hut, dropped to his knees and began confessing to God his sins of temper and irritability against his wife. In the middle of his confession he was interrupted by a still, small voice from within saying, "Norman, don't tell me. I told you. Go and tell your wife."[1]

What an illustration of the truth James tries to convey to his readers when he says, "Therefore confess your sins to one another, and pray for one another, that you may be healed."

The kind of healing James is talking about is wholeness for the whole person. Not just release from physical pain or recovery from bodily illness. But wholeness for the total person, the kind of wholeness that majors on spiritual and emotional health. In other words, the kind of wholeness we need most if we would win over the weariness we feel and the fatigue we fight. James claims there are two steps that must be taken before that kind of total wholeness becomes a reality in our lives: *"confess your sins to one another,"* and *"pray for one another."*

The corollary of that statement is obvious. If we do not confess our sins to one another, we will not be healed. We will not experience the kind of emotional/spiritual wholeness that James claims is ours to experience, the kind of wholeness those Ugandan Christians exhibited.

Pray for One Another

Now we are quite familiar with the second step on the highway to wholeness, *praying for one another.* We know that our prayers for one another really do convey God's healing grace to those for whom we pray. Recently a family in our church was passing through a soul-wrenching experience of profound personal pain. Some of our people knew about it and they prayed earnestly for them. They were actively involved with them in their pain. I had the opportunity to observe the effects of the prayers on that family. God's healing grace broke over them in the throes of their heartache. He did not give them what they wanted. Instead He gave them a strong measure of His wholeness, largely because of fervent prayers that were voiced on their behalf.

Experiences such as this force us to recognize the vital importance of this second step on the highway to healing, that of praying for one another. But what of the first step James mentions here? Namely, confessing our sins to one another. Is this not an exercise that is totally foreign to us? Yet, it is to our detriment that this practice of confessing our sins to one another has fallen into disuse in the church. It is our loss that this discipline has become so foreign to our life together in the Body of Christ. And it is to our shame as Christians that we have left it to the psychiatrists and psychologists to resurrect a shabby secular substitute for this time-honored Christian practice. The practice of confessing one's sins to a select group of confidants within the Body of Christ is a thoroughly biblical, thoroughly Christian discipline, a discipline that has been practiced in the finest epochs of church history.

Confess Your Sins

During the golden age of the Methodist Church, when the ministry of John and Charles Wesley was invading Great Britain with stunning impact, the practice of confessing one's sins to a group of Christian brothers and sisters was widespread. The Wesleys sought some means by which the Holy Spirit might be allowed to perpetuate the new spiritual life that was blossoming in so many. So they organized their converts into groups of about 12 each and called the groups "class meetings."

Each "class" or small group met once a week. And one of the integral elements of those class meetings was a time when each class member would confess his sins of that week to the other members present. That method of personal sharing took the impact of the gospel all the way to the grass roots of British society. And that "method" became one of the key reasons why the Wesleyan movement transformed life in eighteenth-century Great Britain like no other society has been transformed before or since. The Wesleys proved that the first step on the road to emotional/spiritual healing really works for those who dare to work it. Confessing one's sins to a select group of confidants within the body really does communicate wholeness to those who have the courage to try it.

Now, I realize this is a radical principle. Yet I know from personal experience and from biblical authority that we cannot be freed from fears that fatigue us and released from guilt that wearies us until we confess our sins to one another. God wants us to win over our weariness.

In the next chapter I will try to answer the objections you are mulling over in your mind right now—the reasons why you don't confess your sins to your brothers and sisters in Christ, the reasons why you think James' principle is unhealthy and unworkable.

In this chapter I want to share with you three conditions that must be met if the confession of our sins is to bring us the total wholeness James claims it will.

First, confession will bring healing if it is open. The best material being written today on this business of being healed through confession is emerging not from theologians, or Bible scholars, or clergymen, but from psychiatrists and psychologists. One of the best on the contemporary scene is a psychologist in Illinois by the name of O. Hobart Mowrer. In an article entitled, "How to Talk About Your Troubles," Dr. Mowrer laments the unfortunate notion abroad in our society that the only people who can help us in times of severe emotional and spiritual stress are the professional "listeners" in both psychiatry and religion. Mowrer demonstrates how the professional listeners cannot ultimately help us because our confession to them is secret:

> If "secret confession" to priests and psychiatrists had a really good record of accomplishment, we should be glad to be spared the embarrassment of having the "ordinary" people in our lives know who we are. But the record is *not* good; and, reluctantly, many people are today experimenting with *open* confession of one kind or another. When you stop to think of it, *secret confession* is a contradiction in terms. Secrecy is what makes confession necessary. And it is not surprising that the attempt to cope with unresolved personal guilt by means of continued furtiveness does not work out very well. Should we actually expect much to come of letting a priest, minister, psychiatrist, psychologist, social worker or some other "specialist" hear our sins if we continue to live the Big Lie with the people who really matter to us? As a result of my on-going experience with group therapy, both in a mental hospital and in

ordinary community settings, I am persuaded that healing and redemption depend much more upon what we say about ourselves *to others, significant others,* than upon what others (no matter how highly trained or untrained, ordained or unordained) say *to us.* It's the truth we ourselves speak rather than the treatment we receive that heals us.[2]

Isn't this precisely what James claims? "Therefore confess your sins to one another, and pray for one another, that you may be healed."

According to James' inspired insight, our emotional/spiritual healing begins the moment we confess our sins openly to a select group of Christian brothers and sisters.

According to Mowrer, "It's the truth we ourselves speak rather than the treatment we receive that heals us." Both men are bearing witness to the same truth. One from the inspired setting of biblical revelation. The other from a secular setting of contemporary psychology. Yet all truth is God's truth. So here is indisputable truth invading us from two very different sources.

In another place Mowrer restates this truth in these words: "What is clearly needed . . . is the determination and strength to admit, to the 'significant others' in our lives, the exact nature of our wrongs—and then to get about the business of correcting them."[3]

What are the apostle James and Hobart Mowrer trying to tell us? They are trying to say that secret confession will never bring total wholeness to a sinner. Whether that secret confession be voiced to God in prayer, to a priest behind a black curtain or to a professional counselor, it is not sufficient to convey a sense of complete healing to the sinner doing the confessing.

Total wholeness invades our soul and spirit only when we confess our sins to God in the presence of those significant other people in our lives who should hear that confession. Confession that breaks the shroud of our secrecy and leads us out into the open before God and a group of significant other people will liberate us from fear and guilt in a way that nothing else can.

Psalm 51 is a prayer of David. As a prayer it is obviously directed toward God. In this prayer David confesses his twin sins of adultery and murder. But he does not confess them in secret. The very fact that we can read this prayer today is convincing evidence of the fact that David's confession was open. The whole nation knew of his sins. Therefore, the whole nation heard his confession as he voiced it to God and to His people openly and contritely. And it was David's open confession before God and the people that brought him the kind of total wholeness he describes in later psalms. That is what James is trying to tell us. The first condition that will bring healing through confession is openness.

Second, confession will bring healing if it is personal. Notice the word "your" in the text, "Therefore confess *your* sins to one another." With that significant little word "your," James says that your experience of total wholeness hinges on whether or not your confession is personal. That is, whether or not you confess *your* sins. All of us are experts at confessing other people's sins. That is what Watergate was all about. And the country lapped up every last morsel of dirt our news media exposed in Washington. That is what gossip is all about: confessing other people's sins. That is what criticism is all about: airing someone else's faults. That is what blaming is all about: focusing on someone else's failures. We are all experts at confessing other people's sins, exposing other people's dirt, airing other people's faults and focusing on other people's failures. But none of that brings healing. Gossip, criticism and blaming actually drive us further and further away from healing with each fresh indulgence.

Hobart Mowrer tells of two patients newly admitted to the psychiatric ward of the hospital where he works:

> The one spoke at length about how she had been "railroaded" into the hospital, how everyone was against her, and what a blameless life she herself had led. When we eventually asked the next woman how she happened to be in the hospital, she replied simply, "I goofed." Is it difficult to predict which of these two women is going to leave the hospital first? There is, in fact, a real possibility that the first woman may never leave it.[4]

Your experience of wholeness hinges on your willingness to make your confession personal. They are *your* sins. They must be confessed as *your* sins. And when they are, healing is on the way.

Finally, confession will bring healing if it is contrite. Our confession must first be open, then per-

129

sonal, and then contrite. By contrite, I mean "giving evidence of genuine repentance," "demonstrating authentic remorse" for the sins we are confessing. Contrition means a "crushed spirit."

The Hollywood scene is loaded with many stars who are quite willing to air all of their sins for public consumption. Some of them make their living off their reputation as blatant sinners. They confess their sins openly and personally. The sins they exhibit are their own, and they are exhibited for all the world to see. Yet the open, personal exhibition of their sins does not bring Christ's healing to their souls.

Why not? Because there is no contrition in their confession. There is no trace of remorse, no evidence of any repentance. Theirs is an exhibition, not a confession. And there is a profound difference between those two worlds.

Confession must ultimately be contrite. When our spirit is crushed by the consciousness of what we have done, and when our will is prepared to turn around and go the other way—God's way—our confession is contrite. And our contrition brings God's total healing for our troubled soul and our guilty spirit.

Wholeness Personified

The one man alive today who, in my judgment, personifies these three conditions for wholeness better than anyone else is Alexandr Solzhenitsyn. In his books Solzhenitsyn confesses the many flagrant sins of his Russian leaders during the past 60 years. And Solzhenitsyn's writings would be dismissed as muck raking self-pity were it not for his willingness to confess his own sins openly, personally and contritely. In my opinion, *The Gulag Archipelago* delivers such a compelling indictment against Russia's leaders because of those passages where Solzhenitsyn tells the truth about himself with genuine remorse and repentance. Let me quote this excerpt:

> I recall with shame an incident I observed during the liquidation—in other words, the plundering—of the Bobruisk encirclement, when I was walking along the highway among wrecked and overturned German automobiles, and a wealth of booty lay scattered everywhere.... Then I heard a cry for help: "Mr. Captain! Mr. Captain!" A prisoner on foot in German britches was crying out to me in pure Russian. He was naked from the waist up, and his face, chest, shoulders and back were all bloody, while a sergeant osobist, a Security man, seated on a horse, drove him forward with a whip, pushing him with his horse.
>
> He kept lashing that naked back up and down with the whip, without letting him turn around, without letting him ask for help. He drove him along, beating and beating him, raising new crimson welts on his skin .... Any officer, possessing any authority, in any army on earth ought to have stopped that senseless torture. In any army on earth, yes, but in ours? ... So *I was afraid* to defend the Vlasov man against the osobist. *I said nothing and I did nothing. I passed him by as if I could not hear him* .... So the osobist con-

tinued to lash the defenseless man brutally and drive him along like a beast. This picture will remain etched in my mind forever. This, after all, is almost a symbol of the Archipelago. It ought to be on the jacket of this book.[5]

That is confession that counts, confession that brings the kind of healing James is talking about. It communicates wholeness to the sinner because it is open, personal and contrite. Do you want to be healed? Do you really want Christ to free you from your fears, release you from your guilt and deliver you from your fatigue? Then confess your sins openly, personally and contritely to Him in the presence of some people who really care for you. Amen!

Notes

1. Bruce Larson, *No Longer Strangers* (Waco: Word Books, 1971), p. 69.
2. O. Hobart Mowrer, "How to Talk About Your Troubles," *Groups that Work*, ed. Walden Howard (Grand Rapids: Zondervan Publishing House, 1967), p. 107.
3. Mowrer, "How to Talk . . . ," p. 106.
4. Mowrer, 'How to Talk . . . ," p. 109.
5. Alexandr Solzhenitsyn, *The Gulag Archipelago* I and II (New York: Harper and Row Publishers, Inc., 1973), pp. 156, 157.

ROADBLOCKS TO REALITY

> Therefore confess your sins to one another,
> and pray for one another, that you may be
> healed. The prayer of a righteous man has
> great power in its effect (Jas. 5:16).

A Roman Catholic church on the West Coast was having particular difficulty. In fact, it was dying. So a young priest was assigned the task of changing the direction of that perishing church by resurrecting some life within its walls. He accepted that challenge. And within six months he had transformed that loser into a winner by doubling the attendance and tripling the income. This dramatic turn of events caught the bishop's eye. So he paid the church a visit and spent one entire day studying the program the young priest had inaugurated there. At the end of the day he confronted the priest and addressed to him these words:

> My son, I appreciate your efforts to make
> this church a place of relevance. I don't mind
> bucket seats in the sanctuary. I have no dif-
> ficulty tolerating holy water out of electric
> fountains. I don't even object to a drive-in
> confessional booth. But boy that sign you've

got over the booth has got to come down. I mean the one that reads, "Toot and tell, or you'll go to hell."[1]

When the apostle James exhorts us to confess our sins to one another, he is not talking about something as trite as tooting and telling. In the previous chapter we took a close look at what James meant by that command. We noted three things about the kind of confession to which he is referring—confession that is open, personal and contrite. That kind of confession brings God's gift of wholeness to the confessor.

Now, I realize this business of confessing our sins to one another is "heavy stuff." Never do I see more discomfort registered on my listeners' faces than when I speak on this subject. What I see is a mixture of misunderstanding, confusion and outright fear. We hear with our feelings, not with our ears. Therefore, in spite of what the New Testament says about confessing to one another, if we don't feel good about it, we won't hear it and won't buy it. And all who don't buy it have good reasons for their objections. I have boiled down the many objections to two.

Our Fear of Hurting Others

Our first objection to the New Testament's teaching on confession is rooted in our fear of hurting others. Briefly stated, this objection runs as follows. What right do I have to risk another person's peace of mind by confessing my sins to that person? Even if confession is good for my soul, is it necessarily good for the one to whom I confess? Do I have any right to rid myself of guilt feelings at someone else's expense?

134

Now, there is real validity in this concern for other people. Jesus, in Matthew 10:16, commanded His followers to be "wise as serpents and harmless as doves." Therefore, we do well to be wise in selecting the time, the place and the person or persons to whom we confess our sins, lest we inflict unnecessary harm upon them.

Just recently a person in our congregation drew my attention to a situation in which a man's confession to his wife landed her in a mental hospital. Examples such as that force us to step back and take a long, hard look at the value of confession to one another, regardless of what the New Testament says.

I empathize deeply with the heartrending sorrow of that man and his wife. Yet I am not prepared to let extreme examples tempt me to abandon the New Testament's teaching on confession. We must never allow experiences, no matter how convincing or extreme—be they positive or negative—to precede, predominate or preempt the teaching of the New Testament. And the New Testament comes through loud and clear on this matter.

The only way we can find freedom from our fears and release from our guilt feelings is by confessing our sins to God in the presence of those who should hear that confession. Sure there are risks involved, serious risks sometimes.

When we decide to deal honestly with our sins in open, personal, contrite confession, complications can arise. But, in the vast majority of cases, the pluses far outweigh the minuses. The gains far outdistance the losses. The cure far outflanks the complications. The remedy far out-measures the risks. One woman's reaction to her husband's confession of infidelity was more or less typical: "What a mess! But at least now I know the truth."[2] And on that truth she and her husband began building a new life together.

That's the point, isn't it? Any relationship worth its salt must be built on truth. This woman was speaking for a host of others just like her. Though they are hurt by the truth that is confessed to them, they are willing to absorb the hurt because of the privilege of knowing the truth and building on the truth. The primary reason why so many of our interpersonal relationships are not growing or going anywhere is that they are not founded on the truth about us. Therefore, anyone who wants a relationship to grow and go somewhere positive—anyone who longs to see a relationship restored and rejuvenated—welcomes the truth despite the hurt. Because the truth, and only the truth, is sufficient foundation on which to build and rebuild.

I admit that I have no right to rid myself of guilt feelings at someone else's expense if that is all I am doing. But if, by my confession, I am seeking to rebuild a relationship that has been torn, worn, bruised and broken by my duplicity, then I must confess. I must tell that person the truth about me. For that is the only key which will unlock the door to a restored relationship. I confess my sins to that person, not to hurt him, but to enter into a relationship of accountability with him.

From the moment of confession, that person holds me accountable for any restitution that should result from my sins. He holds me accountable for mending my ways and changing my course.

And I hold him accountable for communicating

God's forgiveness to me (see John 20:23). I hold him accountable for praying for me regularly, that I may gain victory over the sins I confess. This is the kind of relationship into which James commissions us to enter with each other when he says, "Therefore confess your sins to one another, and pray for one another, that you may be healed."

I am to confess my sins to you and you are to pray for me. Then you are to confess your sins to me and I am to pray for you. And to those who enter into that relationship of mutual accountability, the Word of God promises healing. Though we may hurt each other at first, ultimately we will heal each other because our new life together will be built on truth.

Our Fear of Hurting Ourselves

Our second objection to the New Testament's teaching on confession is rooted in our fear of hurting ourselves.

Dear Abby and her sister, Ann Landers, in their counsel to millions in the daily newspapers, insist that their troubled readers let bygones be bygones. Whatever you do, don't dredge up your past. Let a sleeping dog lie. Push those ugly skeletons back into the closet and forget them. Why? Because your confession will only hurt you and those whom you love. There's nothing to be gained by it.

In his latest book entitled, *Spandau: The Secret Diaries*, Albert Speer toys with the same conclusion. Even though Speer was Adolph Hitler's master technocrat of the Nazi war effort, in the final year of the war, Speer turned against Hitler and countermanded many of his most destructive orders, thereby saving the lives of thousands if not millions of people. Yet at the Nuremberg trials, he accepted full responsibility for his part in the Nazi war crimes, confessing his sins openly, personally and contritely before the watching and listening world. Despite Speer's confession at Nuremberg, he was sentenced to 20 years' solitary confinement at Spandau Prison with six other Nazi war criminals.

But as Speer writes his diary of those 20 empty years in Spandau, he is noticeably angry that three of his 22 codefendants at Nuremberg were acquitted. Of their acquittal he writes, "So lies, smoke-screens and dissembling statements have paid off after all."[3] Albert Speer claims he has been hurt by his confession. He gained nothing from it. Yet in the same book he tells how his confession enabled him to come to terms with his guilt. Whereas some of his "lucky" codefendants who lied have paid the price of insanity.

Is there, then, any real question about who gained and who lost at Nuremberg? Albert Speer, who confessed his sins and spent 20 years in Spandau Prison, or his "lucky" codefendants who were acquitted by lies and who, with the passing of years, found no way to handle their guilt except by retreating into insanity?

Albert Speer can teach us a lesson about our own fears. We fear to confess our sins to one another because of the danger of hurting ourselves. Yet little do we realize that our refusal to confess our sins—our failure to admit the truth about ourselves—is hurting us much, much more. Think, for a moment, of the worst that can happen to you if you confess your sins. The worst that can befall you is that people might reject you. And that would be a terrible blow to your pride.

But what kind of people would reject you if you confessed your sins to them? What sort of people would wrap their self-righteous skirts around them and walk out of your life? What brand of people would throw your sins back in your teeth or hold them over your head, punishing you with them? Only those who have no sins of their own to confess. Only those judgmental, censorious, better-than-thou, wrist-slapping, finger-pointing sick people who have an emotional need to criticize and castigate others to keep the spotlight off themselves.

Alone with Your Sin

You won't find many of those sick people in your circle of friends. Most of your friends are sinners just like you. And just like you, many of them are alone with their sins. Moreover, many of them would welcome the opportunity to get with you, personally or in a small group, to confess their sins to you and to hear your confession, so that God's wholeness may come to all involved.

Dietrich Bonhoeffer put it better than anyone else I have read on the subject. The following is an extended quotation from Bonhoeffer's book, *Life Together*. Though he wrote this in the 1930s, it is something we need to hear in the 1970s.

> He who is alone with his sin is utterly alone. It may be that Christians, notwithstanding corporate worship, common prayer, and all their fellowship in service, may still be left to their loneliness. The final break-

through to fellowship does not occur, because, though they have fellowship with one another as believers and as devout people, they do not have fellowship as the undevout, as sinners. The pious fellowship permits no one to be a sinner. So everybody must conceal his sin from himself and from the fellowship. We dare not be sinners. Many Christians are unthinkably horrified when a real sinner is suddenly discovered among the righteous. So we remain alone with our sin, living in lies and hypocrisy. . . .

In confession the breakthrough to community takes place. Sin demands to have a man by himself. It withdraws him from the community. The more isolated a person is, the more destructive will be the power of sin over him, and the more deeply he becomes involved in it, the more disastrous is his isolation. Sin wants to remain unknown. It shuns the light. In the darkness of the unexpressed it poisons the whole being of a person. This can happen even in the midst of a pious community. In confession the light of the gospel breaks into the darkness and seclusion of the heart. The sin must be brought into the light. The unexpressed must be openly spoken and acknowledged. All that is secret and hidden is made manifest. It is a hard struggle until the sin is openly admitted. But God breaks gates of brass and bars of iron.

Since the confession of sin is made in the

presence of a Christian brother, the last
stronghold of self-justification is abandoned.
The sinner surrenders; he gives up all his evil.
He gives his heart to God, and he finds the
forgiveness of all his sin in the fellowship of
Jesus Christ and his brother.[4]

Loneliness is definitely the most haunting characteristic of our age. In a "Peanuts" cartoon, Charlie Brown is asked what he will be when he grows up. He answers, "Lonely!"

Loneliness is feared by nearly everyone, and the worst loneliness of all is to be alone with your sin—to be alone in the secrecy of your sin—to be carrying sins you have never given over to Christ in the presence of a brother or sister. Of all forms of loneliness, this one is the most destructive. Whatever you do, don't hesitate to confess your sins to Christ in the presence of a brother or sister because you fear that confession will hurt you. It can only help you. Because it will bring healing to your troubled conscience and joy to your weary soul.

Notes

1. Source unknown.
2. Hobart Mowrer, "How to Talk About Your Troubles," *Groups that Work*, ed. Walden Howard (Grand Rapids: Zondervan Publishing House, 1967), p. 113.
3. Albert Speer, *Spandau: The Secret Diaries* (New York: Pocket Books, 1972), p. 3.
4. Dietrich Bonhoeffer, *Life Together*, trans. John W. Doberstein (New York: Harper and Row Publishers, Inc., 1954), pp. 110-112. Used by permission.

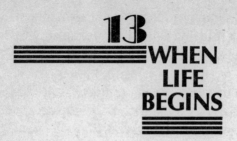

13

WHEN
LIFE
BEGINS

In this the love of God was made manifest among us, that God sent his only Son into the world, so that we might live through him (1 John 4:9).

The thief comes only to steal and kill and destroy; I came that they may have life, and have it abundantly (John 10:10).

It was during the investigation of a bomb threat at the St. Louis airport. Their takeoff had been delayed five hours. So Ann Kiemel and the businessman seated next to her struck up a conversation. And during that conversation Ann found a very natural way to tell him of her relationship with Jesus Christ. After listening to her for a while, that suave, sophisticated man of the world threw his head back and roared with laughter, saying, "You're the first Christian I ever met who makes it sound real and exciting."[1]

Real and exciting! Christianity is that. Not long faces and sad eyes. Not pious prayers and pompous ritual. Not wrist-slapping restrictions and finger-pointing judgment. But life!! Real and exciting life. At least that is the way the New Testament portrays Christianity.

The apostle John's favorite synonym for Christianity is *life*—Life with a capital L. John uses the word "life" incessantly in his writing. It is the word that best captures the meaning of Christ's message as John portrays it. In his first letter he says, "In this the love of God was made manifest among us, that God sent his only Son into the world, so that we might *live* through him" (1 John 4:9).

Earlier in his Gospel, John had penned these words from the lips of Jesus: "I came that they might have *life*, and have it more abundantly" (see John 10:10).

Life in all its abundance. That's what Christianity meant to John. What does Christianity mean to you? Is it real and exciting? Drab and dull? Or neutral and nauseating? John has something to say about life both to the Christian and the non-Christian. Both to the believer and the unbeliever, the insider and the outsider. And what he says about life bears directly upon our ability to win over weariness.

Message to the Unbeliever

To the non-Christian—to the person who has never been born into the family of God through surrender to Jesus—to the one who has never made Jesus his Lord and Saviour through a personal act of commitment—John says, "You're dead!" He doesn't say, "Bang, bang, you're dead." No need for the bang, bang. He just says, "You're dead!"

The New Testament emphasizes the fact that life

begins at the cross of Christ. Life doesn't begin at birth. It begins at new birth. Life doesn't begin at 20 or 40 or 80. Life begins the moment I surrender control of myself to the Christ who came to die that I might live. That is what John means when he says that "God sent His only Son into the world so that we might live through Him." The obvious implication of this statement is that without Christ we have no life. Without Christ we are dead long before we die.

They were saying their bedtime prayers together, Lloyd Ogilvie and his young son. When his turn came, the boy launched into the traditional, "Now I lay me down to sleep, I pray the Lord my soul to keep."

But he was extremely exhausted that night. And when he reached the third line, his tiredness caused him to garble the words. So instead of the usual, "If I should die before I wake," it came out, "If I should wake before I die."[2]

If I wake before I die. That is the essential question of life. Will I awaken before my last breath is taken? The New Testament tells me I am asleep in the darkness of my sin until I claim Christ's death on the cross as my only path to life. I am dead in my selfishness and sin until I let God transfer my death to Christ and His life to me through my personal surrender to Christ.

The story is told of a wealthy man who decreed that when he died he was to be buried in his gold Cadillac. The word got around and when the day came, the crowds gathered to watch as the gold Cadillac was lowered by crane into the grave. And sure enough, there he was, the dead man perched in the driver's seat, with white-gloved hands on the wheel. As the Cadillac disappeared slowly into the grave, one bystander was heard to whisper to another, "Man, that's livin'!"[3]

But that's not livin', is it? That's dyin'. That's not life. That's death. The reason God sent His Son into our world was to bring God's life into our world of death.

You might resist John's line of reasoning and argue, "Look at me! I'm not dead. I am very much alive. I'm a living, breathing, pulsating, thriving, driving, striving human being. My heart is beating. My brain waves are waving. My whole being is throbbing with life." The apostle John would agree with you wholeheartedly.

You are alive clinically. You certainly are a living, breathing, pulsating, thriving, driving, striving human being whose heart is beating and whose brain waves are waving. But that is merely a description of clinical life, functional existence.

John is talking about a totally different kind of life. In John's day, the Greek language was universal. It was spoken everywhere throughout the known world. In the Greek language, there are two different words for "life." The one is *bios* from which we get our word biology. The other is *zoé* from which we get our word zoology. *Bios* means biological existence, clinical life, flesh and blood functional existence, the kind of life described above.

But the good news of the New Testament is that God made a totally different kind of life available to us through Christ. That distinctively different kind of life is described by the New Testament word *zoé*. *Zoé* refers to qualitative life in contrast to clinical life. It has to do with life in a totally new and distinct dimension. Not just clinical existence, but qualitative life, eternal life, God's life breathed into a human soul.

Apart from your personal acceptance of this distinctly new, qualitative life through Christ, you are dead. You have no life. You may well be living, breathing and pulsating with clinical efficiency. All of your biological faculties may be functioning perfectly.

But biological efficiency does not qualify you for life. Life does not begin at biological birth. Life begins at spiritual rebirth. Life begins the moment God's *zoé* enters your inner being in response to your commitment to the Christ who died to make His new life available to you.

The basic difference between animals and humans is that animals can find fulfillment at the level of biological existence, but humans cannot. Animals look down for their fulfillment—to sex, sustenance and survival—and they are satisfied, satisfied on a purely biological plane of existence.

But if man looks down to sex, sustenance and survival for his ultimate fulfillment, he is frustrated, unsatisfied and finally disillusioned. Why? Because man cannot find fulfillment on a purely biological plane of existence.

In a "Peanuts" comic strip, Charles Schulz shows Snoopy on his doghouse sighing, "My life has no meaning. Everything seems empty . . . . I search the skies, but I can find no meaning! No meaning." Suddenly Charlie Brown appears with a dish of dog food, and Snoopy leaps up and shouts, "Ah! Meaning!"[4]

What a graphic portrait of the truth we have before us. Snoopy can find meaning, satisfaction and fulfillment in food. We cannot. Satisfying the clinical demands of our biological existence does not bring us fulfillment. We find our ultimate fulfillment not by looking down to the biological plane of sex, sustenance and survival, but by looking up to the qualitative plane of new, spiritual life God makes available to us through Christ's death on the cross.

St. Augustine said it all when he prayed, "O Lord, Thou hast made us for Thyself, and we are restless until we find our rest in Thee."

How true! We are living at a time when our nation and our world are experiencing a profound, painful sense of restlessness. Why is our world, our culture, our society so restless? Why are so many modern families in chaos? Why are so many individuals beside themselves with disillusionment and despair? Because modern man is looking down to the plane of biological existence for ultimate fulfillment. But no ultimate satisfaction can be found at the clinical level. Why not? Because God made us for Himself. And we will be restless until we find our rest in Him. We will be lifeless, hopeless and frustrated until we receive His gift of qualitative, new life through our personal surrender to the Christ who was sent to bring us that new life.

Take a fish out of water, lay him up on the beach, and then go and talk to that fish while he is involved in a struggle for survival, fighting to exist moment by moment. That fish may give you an elaborate discourse on why he prefers the beach to the water and why he feels it is totally necessary to his self-expression and creativity to be on that beach. He may even try to argue that the water doesn't exist. That's all well and good. But you can bet your bottom dollar that fish is hurting. And he is going to keep on hurting until he gets back into the water.[5]

By the same token, we were made for life with God. We were created to mirror the image of God, to breathe in the new life which comes only from God through Christ. And we are going to be hurting with a painful restlessness until we find our rest in God, until we open our lives to Christ and let Him fill us with His new, qualitative life.

How do we do that? It is really very simple. Something even a child can do. To receive God's gift of new life involves three steps:

First, we must admit to God that we are dead— dead in our selfishness and sin, and totally without hope of generating any new, spiritual life on our own.

Second, we must realize that God knows about our deadness. And because of His overwhelming love for us, He sent His only Son to the cross to die for our sins, that our death might be transferred to Him and His life might be transferred to us.

And finally, we can take personal advantage of what Christ has done for us by claiming His death as our personal path to life and by committing ourselves to Christ as our Saviour and Lord. Have you ever made that commitment? You can do it now, in a brief prayer using these three simple steps. Will you do it?

John says, "In this the love of God was made manifest among us, that God sent his only Son into the world, so that we might *live* through him." To the unbeliever John says, "You're dead! And you need

God's gift of new life through Jesus Christ."

Message to the Believer

To the Christian, to the person who has been born
into the family of God through surrender to Jesus, to
the one who has made Jesus his Lord and Saviour
through a personal act of commitment, to the one
who is following Christ faithfully today, John says,
"You're alive! Now live as though you are alive with
Christ's new life!"

An exasperated waitress approached a couple of
tired businessmen at the lunch counter in Washington National Airport and growled, "Wa'd ya want?"
One of the men looked up and said, "Lady, I want a
slice of life!" To this the waitress slammed down the
menu and replied, "Buddy, that's one thing I ain't got
to give."[6]

A slice of life! Life is the one thing Christians have
that they can give. Life—not just a slice—but new,
abundant life in Christ. John claims God sent Jesus
to give us life. Our challenge, after receiving His new
life, is to live as people who are really alive. I like the
little girl who prayed, "O Lord, make the bad people
good, and please make the good people happy."[7]

How sad that she should have to ask God to make
His good people, His new people, happy. Those of us
who have received Christ's new life are candidates
for happiness. We, of all people, have the total potential for fulfillment, satisfaction and happiness in life.

When I talk to people about this new life in Christ,
I am always very cautious lest I oversell it. I don't
want anyone to think I'm claiming that Christ's new
life solves all one's problems; not by a long shot.

Sometimes total commitment to Christ creates new and difficult problems we never faced before, problems such as dealing with an awakened conscience or making restitution for our wrongs or experiencing rejection from the old crowd or loving people who are easy to hate.

Commitment to Christ does not give you freedom from problems. What it does give you, though, is a new power to cope with your problems. Christians are plagued with problems just as non-Christians are. However, the distinctive difference is that a Christian possesses Christ's new life within. That gives him the power to roll with the punch, to dip with the difficulty and to live as a person who is truly alive. And that is the reason why Christians who have learned to cope with severe problems in their lives are the most alive Christians we have ever met.

One of the most alive and lively persons I ever knew was Edith Pierson, an 88-year-old cripple who passed on to her reward two years ago. When I knew her, Edith was a resident in a retirement home in our community. I made a practice of calling there on a regular basis and occasionally I took our son John along. The incident to which I refer happened when Johnny was about three.

As we walked down the corridor of that infirmary, we stopped at an open door and greeted a lady who was seated in a wheelchair, bent over a table, trying to write with the most horribly deformed hands I had ever seen. She invited us in. Johnny took one look at her and said, "Dad, does she ever have funny-looking hands!"

I hoped she hadn't heard him. But she had, and she

replied, "Yes, I do, don't I? And look at my feet. They're even funnier!" We looked down and saw two shriveled hunks of flesh that used to be feet.

In our subsequent visits together, Edith told me her story. Growing up in Chicago she completed her schooling, took a job with the telephone company, and began to work her way up the corporation ladder until she became manager of a large number of employees. Then, in the prime of her career arthritis hit her with a vengeance and began to cripple her limbs, crush her spirit and smash her dreams. In short order her spiraling career in management was exchanged for a nightmare in a wheelchair. At first she did what we would expect. She became bitter, sour, cynical and filled to the brim with self-pity, hatred, resentment and hostility. Although still professing faith in Jesus Christ, she could not reconcile herself to her awful fate.

Then she changed. After two years of wallowing in her misery, watching her attitude degenerate from awful to unbearable, she did something about it. She decided to take seriously the claims of Scripture that Jesus Christ was actually living in her crippled, shriveling body. So she began to let her awareness of Christ's new life soak into that part of her being where attitudes are formed. She applied His power to change her attitude, to accept her lot, even to thank Him for it, and to make herself available to Him in any way He might be able to use her.

When I knew her, 45 years after arthritis had smashed her, Edith was a veritable dynamo of life. Her beautiful, positive spirit of love was a legend in that community. Her joy was contagious, her disposi-

151

tion vivacious. And although confined to that wheelchair until her dying day, she spent most of her waking hours moving that beautiful right hand of hers across paper—scratching out letters to missionaries—spreading her cheer and sharing her love. And she had a lot of love to share because she shared a lot with me.

That's life! Life that's real and exciting! Life in all its abundance! The kind of new, qualitative life that God sent Jesus to bring to people like us who were imprisoned in mere clinical, biological existence. Christ died to give us life, His life.

Have you received that life? If you haven't, you can. If you have, then live! Live as a person who has been made alive, really alive, by Christ's new life!

Notes

1. Ann Kiemel, *I Love the Word Impossible* (Wheaton: Tyndale House Publishers, 1976), p. 17.
2. Lloyd John Ogilvie, *If I Should Wake Before I Die* (Glendale, Calif.: Regal Books, 1974).
3. Robert Raines, *Success Is a Moving Target* (Waco: Word Books, 1975), p. 14.
4. Charles Schulz, United Features Syndicate, Inc. (January 13, 1974). This cartoon is also featured in *Peanuts Jubilee* (New York: Ballantine Books, 1975), p. 183.
5. R.C. Sproul used this illustration in his clinic on Visitation Evangelism at College Hill Presbyterian Church, Cincinnati, Ohio.
6. Lloyd John Ogilvie, *Let God Love You* (Waco: Word Books, 1974), p. 32.
7. Benjamin Garrison, *Seven Questions Jesus Asked* (Nashville: Abingdon Press, 1975), p. 35.

14
LET
GOD'S LOVE GET
THROUGH TO YOU

For God so loved the world that he gave his
only Son, that whoever believes in him
should not perish but have eternal life (John
3:16).

In 1960 a famous European theologian toured
America. During the question-answer session following his lecture in Chicago, he was asked, "What is the
greatest theological truth you have discovered in
your many decades of study?" A solemn hush fell
over the crowd. Everyone held his breath and listened intently for the profound answer from the aged
scholar. Then came the reply. "The greatest truth I
have been privileged to learn is, 'Jesus loves me this
I know, for the Bible tells me so!' "[1]
How true! Though you live to a hundred, travel the
world and talk to every guru, every wise man, every
holy man, every theologian and scholar, though you
study your Bible night and day until you can recite
it backwards and forwards, you will never uncover
any information even remotely close to the signifi-
cance of this tremendous truth that God loves you.

God loves you! God *loves* you! God loves *you*! He really does.

In *Oldtown Folks*, Henry says, "Once penetrate any human soul with the full belief that God loves him, and you save him."[2]

Total transformation begins to take place in a person when that person lets this tremendous truth soak down into that part of his inner being where he thinks, chooses, feels and really lives. Penetrate any person with the good news that God loves him, and that person becomes a candidate for radical inner revolution.

Dwight Lyman Moody bears strong witness to the impact of this truth in his life. One hundred years ago, D.L. Moody was a rising star in the evangelical church in America. He was pastor of a prominent church in Chicago and an evangelist in increasing demand. But Moody's message was laced with heavy emphasis on hell, damnation and judgment. The only emotions his preaching ever touched in the lives of his listeners were fear and guilt.

Then Moody met an Englishman by the name of Harry Moorehouse. Moorehouse came to Chicago to preach in two meetings at the church where Moody was pastor. When the congregation heard Moorehouse preach, they asked him to stay and speak each night for a week. The thing that got to them about Moorehouse was neither his brilliance nor his oratory, but his message. For, every night he spoke from the same text, John 3:16: "For God so loved the world that he gave his only Son, that whoever believes in him should not perish but have eternal life."

Moorehouse majored on the love of God. And for

seven nights straight he showed them from the Scriptures how God loved them and what He had done for them through Christ because of His love for them. And in seven short days of exposure to that powerful, positive message of good news, that congregation was transformed.

What is even more significant, their famous pastor was transformed. Four years later, reflecting on that life-changing week with Harry Moorehouse, D.L. Moody wrote:

> I used to preach that God hates the sinner, and seeks to destroy him . . . that God was behind the sinner with a double edged sword, ready to hew him down . . . I never knew . . . that God loved us so much. This heart of mine began to thaw out; I could not hold back the tears. I just drank it in . . . I took up that word "Love," and I do not know how many weeks I spent in studying the passages in which it occurs, till at last I could not help loving people. I had been feeding on love so long that I was anxious to do everybody good . . . I got full of it. It ran out my fingers.[3]

That is what I would like to see happen to you and me. The good news of the New Testament is not that God loves the world. Rather, the good news of the New Testament is that God loves you. He really does. He loves you just as you are with all of your ups and downs, ins and outs, pluses and minuses. He loves you! If God's love is to penetrate your life, and produce this transformation, you must be willing to do two things: *concentrate on the crucified Christ*, and *perforate your defenses.*

Concentrate on the Crucified Christ

Field Marshal Slim was commander of the British troops in Burma during World War II. On one occasion Field Marshal Slim heard that one of his soldiers had received disturbing news from home. His wife was "running around." The young soldier in the swamps of Burma was crushed with despair.

So the field marshal asked the senior chaplain to arrange for a visit with that soldier. The chaplain duly sent one of his men to visit the despondent soldier. And following the visit, Field Marshal Slim sent for the senior chaplain. "Padre," he said, "about that visit I asked you to get one of your chaplains to pay."

"Well, sir," replied the senior chaplain, "what about it?"

"Well, Padre," said Slim, "your chaplain went to see the man. He was very nice to him. He smoked a cigarette with him, and drank a cup of tea with him. But he never showed that soldier the one thing he wanted to see."

"What was that?" asked the senior chaplain. And Slim answered, "The man on the Cross. Padre, when are you going to show us the one thing we want to see—the man on the Cross?"[4]

Why did Field Marshal Slim want his chaplains to show his soldiers "the man on the Cross?" Why did he want this despondent soldier to see "the man on the Cross?" It was because Field Marshal Slim had, by personal experience, come to know the Christ on the cross as the most convincing proof of God's love for him. And he wanted all of his men to share that experience.

That despondent soldier had just received word

that the woman whom he thought loved him really didn't after all. What can possibly revive a heart that has been smashed with raw reality like that? What can possibly breathe warmth and life into a soul made suddenly to feel so cold and dead? What can possibly convince a man feeling so alone, so helpless and so hopeless that, in fact, he is not alone? He is not helpless. Neither is he hopeless. What can possibly grip him with the truth that he is still loved? Certainly not a cigarette, a cup of tea and a few kind words.

The only thing known to man that can convince lonely people that they are not alone, and helpless people that there is hope, broken people that they can be mended is a fresh, personal experience with "the man on the Cross."

God proved His love to us preeminently at the cross. Jesus laid down His life in our place that He might make available to us a personal experience of God's love, God's life, God's help and God's hope. Therefore, the only thing we all need—regardless of our current state of mind and heart—is a long, strong look at the Christ on the cross. For He, more than anything or anyone else, demonstrated God's love for us.

Jesus came into our world to reveal God to us. Therefore, in Jesus we see God. In His actions, words, life, death and resurrection we see what God is like. When Jesus fed the hungry, healed the sick, touched the untouchable and loved the unlovable, He was saying to them and to us across the centuries, "This shows how much I love you." When He endured the insults, injuries, treacheries and disloyalties of both friend and foe, He was saying to them and to us, "Nothing you can do to me will ever stop me from loving you." When Peter denied and Judas betrayed, Jesus treated them in such a way as to say, "Nothing you can do to me will ever stop me from loving you." When they flogged Him, reviled Him, spit on Him, mocked Him and then nailed Him to the cross, Jesus prayed, "Father, forgive them; for they don't know what they do" (Luke 23:34). In that prayer He was saying, "Nothing you can do to me will ever stop me from loving you." It is there on the cross that Jesus showed us the convincing proof of God's love for us.

Had Jesus stopped short of the cross—had He been willing to show us God's love in His life but not in His death—He would have been circumscribing boundaries around God's love for us. He would have been saying, "There is a point beyond which God's love will not go. There is a limit beyond which God's love will not reach. There is a sacrifice which God's love is not prepared to make on your behalf." But by going all the way to the cross, Jesus announced to the world, loud and clear, "There is nothing under the sun that you can do to me that will stop me from loving you. I love you just as you are."

And what Jesus says, God the Father says. Suspended between heaven and earth on that tree of torture Jesus proclaims the illimitable, unconquerable, inexhaustible, love of God. It cost the cross to convince man of the love of God. The pain, agony, loneliness and sin-bearing sacrifice of the cross was the price Jesus had to pay to placard God's love before us in its most compelling display.

God's love for us comes through most convincingly at the cross. Without the cross, His love would not reach us and could not change us. Therefore, if you would be gripped by the positive, powerful, personal conviction that God loves you, you must concentrate on the Christ on the cross. For it is there on the cross that Jesus overwhelms us with the evidence that God loves us.[5]

A North American Indian gave the following witness of his experience of God's love:

> There came to our tribe a man who extolled the God of the white man. We told him to leave. There came another man and he said, "Do not drink any more firewater. Do not get drunk, and do not steal." We paid no attention to him. Then there came a man who told us of a God who loves Indians so much that He came down from heaven to live among us, to walk in our moccasins. This God shared our life and died in our place. His death paid for our sins and opened the doors whereby we might be saved and enter heaven to be with Him forever. And when I heard news like that, I could never forget it.[6]

Why? Because that Indian had been gripped by the good news of a God who loves Indians so much, that He was willing to come and die for them, that His life, His love, His help and His hope might become theirs now and always. The cross of Jesus is where God's love in all of its costliness, its forgiveness, its sacrifice and its limitlessness is seen best. Therefore, if the truth of John 3:16 would penetrate your life, you must concentrate on the Christ on the cross. The cross of Christ is where John's claims about God's love for you take on their most convincing meaning.

Perforate Your Defenses

For God's love to penetrate your life to the level where transformation takes place, you must also perforate your defenses. God's penetration requires perforation as well as concentration.

What do I mean by perforation? Simply this. All of us are engaged in the constant process of erecting elaborate defenses around those areas of our lives where God is not welcome. We build massive dikes in front of certain parts of our lives to dam up the flow of God's love and keep it from penetrating some of the places where we think and feel and live. Therefore, if God's love is ever going to penetrate our lives to the level where transformation takes place, we must be willing to perforate our defenses, to blow holes in our own dikes.

What kind of defenses and dikes? Things like our selfishness and self-centeredness. Things like our destructive emotions of resentment, bitterness, anger, fear and hatred. Things like our negative attitudes, our judgmental spirit, our self-righteous outlook. Things like our sense of self-sufficiency, our pride and self-reliance, our desire to run our own lives.

Earlier in this chapter I underscored the truth that there is nothing you can do to *stop* God from loving you. That is the good news of the New Testament. But there is something you can do to *keep* God's love from getting through to you: You can run away and hide in your deep, dark caves of self-centeredness. You can crawl in behind your walls of defense and your dikes of selfishness. And though God will pursue you relentlessly with His love—though He will dog your steps, track you down and corner you with the warmth of His kindness—He will not beat down your door.

Our God is the eternal Gentleman. He honors your freedom of choice. He respects your right to live without His love if you so desire. If you want His love to transform your life, then you must be willing to stop running and to start opening yourself to Him. One of the awesome truths of the New Testament is that as powerful as God's love is, we have the ability to keep it from getting through to us.

Wallace Hamilton tells of a pastor in a small western town whose son grew up to be rebellious and recalcitrant. Under the father's roof the boy was irritable and unmanageable, contemptuous of his father's faith and even resentful of his mother's kindly concern. One midnight, after years of reaching out to that boy, the father, with heavy heart, stole into his son's bedroom to find the air filled with the fumes of alcohol, and the boy's mother kneeling by his bed, stroking his hair, kissing his forehead, caressing him. Looking up through her tears she said, "He won't let me love him when he's awake."[7]

How much like that boy are many of us in our relationship with God. We won't let Him love us. We keep Him at arm's length. We lock Him out of those areas of our lives where we don't want Him to bug us. We run away and hide from His love in the deep, dark caves of our own self-centeredness.

Francis Thompson was a brilliant poet in nineteenth-century England whose life fell apart emotionally and spiritually, plunging him to skid row. But despite debauchery and drunkenness, he could not drown out the pursuing call of God.

Speaking later of his inability to run away from God, whom he called "The Hound of Heaven," Thompson wrote,

> I fled Him, down the nights and down the days;
> I fled Him, down the arches of the years;
> I fled Him, down the labyrinthine ways
> Of my own mind; and in the mist of tears
> I hid from Him, and under running laughter . . . .
> From those strong Feet that followed,
> followed after.[8]

Finally, after many years, Francis Thompson let "The Hound of Heaven" catch him, change him and charge him with the electricity of His new life and love. And Francis Thompson lived out the remainder of his years as a powerful witness to the God whose love would not let him go.

The same God loves you with the same relentless, persistent, pursuing love today. Do you believe that? Do you really believe that the eternal God of the universe loves somebody like you? The great good news of the New Testament is that God loves you. He really does.

"For God so loved *you* that He gave His only Son. . . . " If only you would be gripped by this positive, powerful, personal truth! Your life would be transformed.

What can you do to make that transformation a reality? What must you do if God's powerful love is to penetrate your life and soak into that level of your inner being where you really think and feel and live? Penetration requires concentration and perforation. First, you must concentrate on the Christ on the cross who shows you convincing proof of God's love for you. Then you must perforate your own stubborn defenses, blow holes in your own strong dikes and let God's love through to you. Isn't it incredible that we should run away from the God who loves us? Will you stop running and let His love come through to you?

Notes

1. Karl Barth at the University of Chicago.
2. Charles Allen, *The Miracle of Love* (Old Tappan, N.J.: Fleming H. Revell Co., 1972), p. 87.
3. D.L. Moody, "The Great Redemption," Chicago, 1889. Quoted by Richard Curtis, *They Called Him Mister Moody* (Grand Rapids: Wm. B. Eerdmans Publishing Co., 1962), p. 134.
4. William Barclay, *A Spiritual Autobiography* (Grand Rapids: Wm. B. Eerdmans Publishing Co., 1975), pp. 70,71.
5. Jesus died on the cross to do much more than display God's love to us. He died as our substitutionary sin-bearer, taking our guilt and God's wrath into Himself on the cross. However, I am focusing this chapter on the cross as the ultimate display of God's love because this truth has the potential to convince people that God really loves them. In this regard, I am deeply indebted to William Barclay's powerful portrait of Jesus as the one who shows us how much God loves us, in *A Spiritual Autobiography* (Grand Rapids: Wm. B. Eerdmans Publishing Co., 1975), pp. 50,51.
6. Adapted from W.A. Criswell, *Expository Sermons on Galatians* (Grand Rapids: Zondervan Publishing House, 1973).
7. Charles Allen, *The Miracle of Love* (Old Tappan, N.J.: Flming H. Revell Co., 1972), pp. 88,89.
8. Francis Thompson, "The Hound of Heaven," *Masterpieces of Religious Verse*, ed. James Morrison (New York: Harper and Row Publishers, 1948), p. 57.

15 GOOD NEWS FOR LOSERS

When the sabbath was past, Mary Magdalene, and Mary the mother of James, and Salome, bought spices, so that they might go and anoint him [Jesus]. And very early on the first day of the week they went to the tomb when the sun had risen. And they were saying to one another, "Who will roll away the stone for us from the door of the tomb?" And looking up, they saw that the stone was rolled back; for it was very large. And entering the tomb, they saw a young man sitting on the right side, dressed in a white robe; and they were amazed. And he said to them, "Do not be amazed; you seek Jesus of Nazareth, who was crucified. He has risen, he is not here; see the place where they laid him. But go, tell his disciples and Peter that he is going before you to Galilee; there you will see him, as he told you" (Mark 16:1-7).

A salesman in downtown Minneapolis hunted in vain for a parking space. To his dismay the lots were all full. Even the parking garages were jammed. So in desperation he left his car in a no-parking zone with this note on the windshield:

> I've circled this block 10 times and have searched high and low. I have an appointment to keep or I'll lose my job. Forgive us for our trespasses.

A police officer happened by a short while later, read the note and left this reply:

> I've circled this block for 20 years. If I don't give you a ticket, I'll lose my job. Lead us not into temptation.[1]

That salesman is every one of us. He is everyone who is painfully conscious of the ground he is losing in the game of life. He is everyone who has been led into temptation, has succumbed to temptation, and who is acutely aware of his many trespasses. And that really includes all of us, doesn't it? In a sense, all of us are losers in one way or another. Thomas Hardy reflected on that fact in his diary when he wrote:

> If all hearts were open, all desires known—as they would be if people showed their souls—how many gapings, sighings, clenched fists, knotted brows, broad grins and red eyes would we see in the market place?[2]

The "walking wounded" are all around us. Possibly you are one of them. Possibly your eyes are red, your brow is knotted, your fist is clenched and your soul is sighing. Possibly you are one of those who knows that everything in his life is not falling into place as it should. If that is the case with you, then take heart. I have good news for you. According to Mark's Gospel, the news of Christ's resurrection is nothing more or less than good news for losers.

When God's messenger announced the news of Christ's resurrection to those three startled women who came to the tomb to embalm Christ's body, he said, "Do not be amazed: you seek Jesus of Nazareth who was crucified. He has risen, he is not here; see the place where they laid him. But go, tell his disciples *and Peter* . . . "

This chapter focuses on that surprising two-word phrase "and Peter." That little phrase is the light at the end of the tunnel for all who would win over weariness. When God's messenger adds those two words to his supremely significant announcement, he is telling us that the news of Christ's resurrection is primarily for losers. *God singles out the loser for His special attention*; he also says that *God sees the loser's possibilities under the rubble of his failures.*

God Looks for Losers

"Go, tell his disciples and Peter." I find that to be truly amazing. God's messenger singles Peter out of the crowd and focuses God's special concern on him in this announcement. Peter was one of the disciples. Why then, did God's messenger commission the women to tell the news of Christ's resurrection to "his disciples and Peter"? What made Peter so special that he should receive the VIP treatment?

If you know the story, the answer is obvious. Peter was a loser. He had blown it badly. Only a few days before, he promised his Lord that though all others forsake Him and run, he would stand his ground (see Matt. 26:33). He vowed, "Lord, I am ready to go with you to prison and to death . . . I will lay down my life for you" (see Luke 22:33; John 13:37).

166

And Peter meant every word of those vows. Was he not the one who that very night whipped out his sword and lopped off the ear of one of the men who had come to arrest Jesus? By so doing Peter put action to his words. He laid his loyalty and his life on the line in that impetuous assault. Yet, while he was ready for the enemy, he was not ready for the strange strategy Jesus used on the enemy. For Jesus reached down, picked up that bloody ear, grafted it back onto the head of the enemy, turned to Peter and said, "Put your sword away, Simon. We don't need that."

When Jesus said that, a cloud of disillusionment enveloped Peter. They took Jesus off to the high priest's kangaroo court, and Peter followed at a distance. He stood within earshot and listened as they marched Jesus through the motions of a mock trial. And what Peter heard caused him to give up. He grumbled to himself, "What's the use? Our cause is finished. Jesus is a goner. There He stands with all the power to wipe them off the face of the earth, and He lets them ride roughshod over Him."

About that time, a young servant girl happened by, overheard Peter's mumbling, recognized his Galilean accent, looked him over carefully and said, "You were one of His followers, weren't you?"

And Peter denied it. He denied it not once but three times; not casually but vehemently; not flippantly, but blasphemously. He reeled off a long string of oaths and curses, turned the air blue with filth. And in the process renounced all knowledge of Jesus of Nazareth. Then, having stunned himself with his own cowardice, he ran out into the night and wept bitterly (see Mark 14:66-72).

That was Thursday night and early Friday morning. Now it is Sunday morning, just after sunrise. And as these three devout women stumble into the open tomb, they are startled speechless by a messenger from God who says, "Do not be amazed; you seek Jesus of Nazareth, who was crucified. He has risen, he is not here; see the place where they laid him. But go, tell his disciples. [And above all, make sure you tell Peter!]"

Why Peter? Had not all of the disciples forsaken Jesus and fled? Yes they had. But Peter, more than any of the others, needed to hear the news personally. They all had become disillusioned and disheartened. But Peter was most despondent. He was crushed by the consciousness of his failure. He was a loser and he knew it and it was really bothering him.

Peter had failed his friend in the clutch. And because of that, he was gouged with guilt. He was suffocating with shame. So God's messenger singled out Peter for special attention. Peter was a loser who knew he was a loser. And God wanted him to know that in the resurrection of His Son, Jesus, hope dawned for Peter and all losers, then and now.

Possibly you feel much more like Peter than like one of the other disciples. Possibly you share Saul Kane's sentiments when he confessed how appalled he was at "the harm I've done by being me."[3] Possibly you are cornered by a confining sense of guilt and shadowed by a strong sense of shame. Possibly you are painfully conscious of the fact that you, like Peter, are a loser. Everything in your life is not falling into place as it should. You have failed miserably, and you know it. You have blown it badly, and you admit it.

If that is so, then cheer up! The good news of Christ's resurrection is tailor-made for you. Your acute awareness of defeat can be the launching pad to a whole new life, just as it was for Peter on that first Easter morning.

Said Archibald MacLeish in his play, *J.B.*:

"It's from the ash heap God is seen.
Always! Always from the ashes.
Every saint and martyr knew that."[4]

Peter was on the ash heap of defeat and despair on that first Easter morning. But God's good news of the risen Christ grabbed Peter, the loser, and transformed him into a mighty winner. And the good news is that the risen, living Christ can do the same for you, no matter how big a loser you may be.

What God asks you to do is to admit that you are losing the game of life without Him. He asks you to acknowledge that you are not putting all the pieces of your puzzle together in your own strength. Then He asks you to surrender your life to Him just as you are, with all of your lumps and bumps, bruises and brokenness. But first you must be willing to admit that without Christ in your life, you are a loser, for "it's from the ash heap God is seen. Always! Always from the ashes."

The resurrection of Christ holds personal meaning only for those losers who know that without Him they lose. Losers who think they can win without Christ find no meaning in the resurrection. They are like the gnat that alighted on a wagon as it was being pulled by a team of horses up a dusty, country road. The gnat looked behind him and exclaimed, "My, what a dust I'm raising!"

169

There are many people in our prosperous nation just like that little gnat. They are riding the highway of success. Everything is coming up roses for them. Life is smooth sailing and easy money. But what they don't realize is that all of their achievements, affluence and joyride to greatness are gifts from a gracious God who loves them and is showering His kindness upon them to lead them to repentance (see Rom. 8:24). He's the one who is "raising the dust" of success in their lives. But they don't see that. All they see is their own greatness—and that makes them losers, losers who think they are winners. People like that find no personal meaning or relevance in the news of Christ's resurrection.

On the other hand, those who cherish the resurrection of Jesus as the cornerstone of their lives are people who are acutely aware of their many sins, their gross failures and their awesome inability to please God with their own "goodness." These are the people who find themselves on the ash heap of personal failure. And from those ashes they cry out to the living Christ who answers their cry, enters their lives and, by His resurrection power, begins to put their pieces back together again.

God Sees Your Possibilities

God sees the loser's possibilities under the rubble of his failures. Did you notice that God's messenger refers to Simon as "Peter"? He says, "Go, tell His disciples *and Peter*." How strange! The man's name was actually Simon. He was Simon the fisherman; Simon, the brother of Andrew. Yet the message of resurrection is sent to "Peter."

"So what?" you say. "What difference does it make what name they call him?" Oh, it makes a lot of difference. Names are very important.

I think of the pastor who had great difficulty with names. One Sunday morning a woman came through the line at the door and asked, "You remember me, don't you?" He didn't. But he thought he'd fake it. So he said, "Oh, yes I do! Now tell me, do you spell your name with an 'e' or an 'i'?" She replied, "With an 'i' and it's Hill."[5] Names are of utmost importance. That is why God's messenger selects the name "Peter" with great precision in this announcement.

Three years previously, when Jesus first met Simon, Jesus said, "You are Simon, the son of John? You shall be called . . . Peter" (John 1:42). The name Peter means "rock." What Jesus was implying in that initial meeting was that though Simon was known then throughout the fishing community of Galilee as "Simon, the son of John," someday, through his association with Jesus, he would be known as "Peter, the rock." Peter, the rock of leadership, of courage, of greatness, of strength.

Is it not startling that God's messenger should choose to use Simon's new name at this time of miserable failure in Simon's life? The messenger refers to him as Peter—"Rocky" at a time when Simon had been anything but a rock. He had acted much more like a mound of yellow Jello. Why then, does God's servant use the name Peter? Is he trying to make a sick joke? Hardly!

God's messenger chooses the name Peter for a particular purpose. A purpose of profound importance! That purpose is to convey the message that He sees the loser's possibilities under the rubble of his failures. God saw Peter—the rock, Peter—the courageous winner, under the rubble of Simon—the coward, Simon—the loser.

What You Can Become

And the good news is that God sees you in the very same light. He does not major on your actualities. He majors on your possibilities. He looks at you not in terms of what you are, but in terms of what you can become under the control of His grace and power. He wants you to let Him apply His resurrection power to your life so that all of the possibilities He sees in you may become realities.

God saw the *promise* in Peter, not the *problems* in Simon. He saw the *courage* in Peter, not the *cowardice* in Simon. He saw the *possibilities* in Peter, not the *actualities* in Simon. He saw the *future* in Peter, not the *past* in Simon. He saw the *greatness* in Peter, not the *smallness* in Simon. So he sent the women after Peter.

The same God sees your promise today, not your problems. He sees your courage, not your cowardice. He sees your possibilities, not your actualities. He sees your future, not your past. He sees your greatness, not your smallness. And He asks you, "Will you give yourself to me, today, lock, stock and barrel? Will you give all of yourself to me? If you will, I will plug your life into the very same power that raised Jesus from the dead. And I will make you everything you can possibly become."

Now, that is an offer too good to refuse. Simon took the Lord up on that offer. And God transformed

Simon into everything Simon could possibly become. By God's grace and power Simon became Peter, the mighty rock. And God promises to do the same with you, if you let Him. He sees all of your possibilities under the rubble of your failures.

Johnny Cash bears convincing witness to the power of the living Christ in his experience. He tried to live his life without Christ. He knew better. He had been raised in a devout Christian home and knew the claims of Christ upon his life. But Johnny Cash was mesmerized by the bright lights of country music and all the accoutrements of big time entertainment. In a few short years he made it big in the big time. His career blossomed with a flourish.

But in the process, Johnny Cash made a sad mess of his life. He was a failure as a husband. His first marriage ended in divorce. He was a failure as a father. Since he was on the road incessantly, his four daughters grew up as strangers to him, and he to them. He was a failure as a man. For seven long years he was enslaved in the darkness of drug addiction. In short, Johnny Cash was a loser.

Yet all during those troubled years he knew God was pursuing him. He sensed that the Lord saw what he could be, not what he was. He knew God was sparing his messed-up life for a special purpose. He knew this because a woman named June Carter kept telling him over and over again, "God has His hand on you, John, and I'm going to help you become what you are whether you want me to or not."[6]

Then one day in 1967, Johnny Cash found himself on the ash heap of life. And for the first time, he admitted his failures. He faced the disgusting truth about himself, stopped running, and surrendered himself to Christ.

In succeeding weeks he underwent a torturous ordeal of withdrawal from drugs. But the risen, living Christ who had entered Cash's broken life, applied His resurrection power to that man's will, and enabled him to "kick the habit." And today, Johnny Cash is a dynamic witness to the power of Christ in a loser's life. By the grace and strength of the living Lord, Cash is becoming the man God saw he could be. His amazing possibilities are now becoming realities under the enabling power of the Christ who lives in his life.

Sensing Your Need

You may not have messed up your life as Johnny Cash did his. You may not be a failure in your marriage. You may not be a failure as a parent. You may not be a failure as a person in the eyes of society. But you may be trapped in the deceptive darkness of your own self-sufficiency. You may be pursuing the fantasy of self-reliance. You may be trying to run your life without Christ. You may be committed to the premise that you can make it quite nicely on your own. Therefore, you do not sense your need of the transforming grace of the risen Christ.

If that is where you are, you are trapped in far deeper darkness than Johnny Cash ever was. For, until you begin to sense the pain of your own inadequacies—until you find yourself on the ash heap of personal insufficiency—the life-changing power of the risen Christ will never become a personal reality to you.

Until you sense your need, God will pursue you with His compelling love. He will dog your steps relentlessly with His kindness, His mercy and His grace, seeking to lead you to the place where you admit you cannot live without Him. For He sees you not as you are but as you can become through the power of the risen Christ. Therefore, He invites you to stop running and to open your life to Him, that He might begin to make you what He knows you can become.

At the Atlanta airport a woman named Frances had just come from the funeral of her youngest sister. As she awaited her flight out of town, she was forlorn and broken with grief. But little did Frances know that God had a surprise in store for her that dark day. He planned to bring across her pain-filled path the vibrant witness of Ann Kiemel.

As Ann came breezing through the terminal she saw Frances sitting off by herself, visibly troubled. So Ann walked over to her, introduced herself and engaged her in conversation. Ann listened intently as Frances began exposing the painful edges of hurt she was feeling. Then Ann shared with her the news of a God who loved people like Frances so much that He was willing to come into her world, lay down His life for her and be raised from the dead that His new life and power might become hers. After hearing this astounding news, Frances said, "Ann, can I tell you this? I'm a high school math teacher. No one likes me. Everyone hates me. They call me all kinds of names, but their favorite is 'old battle-ax' and I deserve every name. But you are the very first person in my life to tell me I am special, that Jesus really cares for me . . . . Ann, is it really true that Jesus can make something beautiful out of my life?"[7]

That is the message of Easter. Jesus Christ, the risen, living Lord of history and eternity can make something beautiful out of your life. He sees you today, not as you are, but as you can become. He sees your possibilities under the rubble of your many failures. He focuses on your future, not on your past. He sees your potential greatness, not your present smallness. He sees it all, and says, "I can make something beautiful out of your life. Will you give me a chance? Will you stop running and surrender yourself to my Son, Jesus? If you will, I will apply His resurrection power to your life."

And He will enable you to win over weariness.

Notes

1. Adapted from Ben Ferguson, *God, I've Got a Problem* (Santa Ana, Calif.: Vision House, Inc., 1974), p. 9.
2. Thomas Hardy, *Diary* (August 18, 1908). Quoted by Robert Montgomery in "The Power of Positive Suffering," *Pulpit Digest* (September 1971), p. 52.
3. John Masefield, "Everlasting Mercy," *Poems* (New York: Macmillan Publishing Co., Inc., 1953).
4. Archibald MacLeish, *J.B.*, Sentry Edition (Boston: Houghton Mifflin Co., 1956), p. 50.
5. Charles McClain, Jr., "To Flee or to Fly," *Pulpit Digest* (July-August 1973), p. 17.
6. Johnny Cash, *The Man in Black* (Grand Rapids: Zondervan Publishing House, 1975), p. 58.
7. Ann Kiemel, *I Love the Word Impossible* (Wheaton: Tyndale House Publishers, 1976), p. 128.